FOREIGN POLICY ANALYSIS

FOREIGN POLICY ANALYSIS

by

FELIKS GROSS

Brooklyn College of the City of New York
and New York University

PREFACE

by

ADOLF A. BERLE JR.
Former Assistant Secretary of State

PHILOSOPHICAL LIBRARY
New York

Printed in the United States of America

To My Parents

Foreword

MAKING and executing foreign policy is perhaps the highest political function of a state. Errors can lead to consequences more destructive than hydrogen bombs. Successes can alleviate the lot or liberate the capacities of millions of individuals. Too often foreign policy has been conceived as a product of the individual genius of men to whom destiny has confided the guidance of nations. In this romantic view, foreign policy has been presented as the creation of Talleyrand or Castlereagh, of Metternich or Bismarck, of Roosevelt, Churchill or Stalin. Execution of foreign policy was thus an art practised by men of stupidity or talent, of stubbornness or genius.

Modern thought tends to reject alike this interpretation, and the method it connotes. Rather, it seeks, painfully, bases for scientific analysis and scientific formulation. One reason for this unquestionably is the considerable twentieth-century expansion of the social sciences. These begin to provide measurement of factors and indications of trend unknown to the statesmen of two centuries ago. Factors constant in any foreign policy, however practised, can now in some degree be isolated, separately examined, and their weight evaluated. In making decisions the area in which pure speculation must be relied on is now reduced: a competent political organization, for example, can have reasonably reliable data on population and population trends, on the economic situation and economic potentials, on military strength and vulnerability, and so forth. The beginnings of a science of measurement of

vii

ideological and psychological forces are at least present. A
desk chief in the Department of State or in the Foreign Office
at Whitehall probably knows more about the factors of every
foreign problem than Canning or Richelieu could possibly
have known about any of the situations on which they were
working.

Probably one result of the modern approach has been oversimplification. It is tantalizingly easy to adopt a single, well
argued and well constructed theory of international relations as a complete answer. All of us have met foreign policy
experts who were content to base their estimates, their syn-
theses and their forecasts on the theories, let us say, of Admiral
Mahan and his hypothesis of sea power, or of Sir Halford Mac-
Kinder and his hypothesis of geopolitics, or of the economic
determinists of a generation past. Most careful students of
foreign policy today reject any single theory, however soundly
it may be based as far as it goes. At best, certain elements only
of international relations have been reduced to scientific
description and analysis. There is no likelihood that *all* elements can be thus isolated and brought under control in the
foreseeable future. But we can, in some measure, divide those
factors in foreign policy which are subject to a degree of
scientific analysis and estimate from those which are not. This
does not, of course, eliminate the chancy element of human
genius, with its capacity for hideous error or for inspired
solution. But at least it reduces somewhat the area of doubt.

So far as I am aware, no prior attempt has been made to
analyze foreign policy and its making in the light of the tools
offered by modern social science. This is the real contribution
which Professor Gross here offers. To the extent that he is
successful, techniques may be constructed by which foreign
policy in the past can be evaluated, and the causes of its success or failure may be ascertained. A like technique applied
to current policy problems should conduce to better appraisal
of the probable effects of any given decision, or line of action.
Professor Gross would, I think, be the last to claim that he had
found any infallible (or even wholly satisfactory) method and
technique. The point is that he has made a start.

For this he is entitled to recognition and to thanks, for the twentieth century is persistently offering us a set of problems in foreign affairs unrivalled in recorded history.

For example, the economic and military techniques and results emerging from the technological revolution have changed the entire basis of so-called "international relations." No nation-state (with the possible but by no means certain exception of the present Sino-Russian complex) is presently able, as an isolated entity, either to support the economic life demanded by its people, or to defend its borders. With this massive fact statesmen in all countries are still wrestling, rather inadequately. Again, roughly half the world is presently organized and operated by a political group which appears to believe individuals are created and designed to serve aggregate organization—whereas for the past three centuries (roughly since the Reformation) the prevailing world considered the individual as the end product of sound civilization. Again the ability to exploit mass myths through mass media of communication has expanded almost beyond calculation: political movements increasingly follow the areas of air-wave radio rather than territorial borders. These are only a few illustrations; they can be greatly multiplied. To know what you are doing and where you will probably arrive in the twentieth century is vastly more difficult than it was when Bismarck provoked and fought a "little war" against France about 1870, or when Disraeli backed the Turks against the Russian Empire in 1878.

A seventeenth century Foreign Minister would have analyzed his problem first in terms of the comparative military force presently available to his opponents and to him, and how he could get it and use it to accomplish a defined national purpose. Professor Gross, writing in the twentieth century, makes the axis of his analysis "ideology," on the ground that foreign policy is a social process and that social processes are dominated by ideology. A late nineteenth century diplomatist would very likely have begun his analysis with a study of economic factors—that being the era in which economic determinism had become fashionable. Your twentieth century analyst down-grades economics to one of several factors of power (power being considered as capacity to produce given results) just as military power is being reduced to a like auxiliary status. For all we know, international relations experts of the twenty-first century will have newer and more penetrating concepts than any dreamed of today.

The contribution of this volume is that it attempts to formulate a method and technique in a field sadly bare of clear ideas on that subject. Whoever tackles that task is entitled to thanks. The respect and the thanks will be deserved in even greater measure if, as a result, other scholars successfully carry the attempt forward in the future.

Adolf A. Berle, Jr.

Table of Contents

CHAPTER   PAGE

FOREWORD   vii

INTRODUCTION   xv

PART 1

I. SCIENTIFIC APPROACH   3
The Scope   3
The Role of a Hypothesis   6
Selection of Facts   10
Values and Facts   16
Operational Method and Method of Analysis   18
Theory   20
Method-Centered and Problem-Centered Approach   21

II. CAUSATION   22
Foreign Policy as a Social Process   22
Conflict and Cooperation   25
Social Causation   27
Monocausal and Pluralistic Approaches   31
Functional-Interactional Approach   35
Alternative Effects   37

III. SEMANTICS AND TERMINOLOGY   39
The Meaning of Words in Foreign Policy   39
What Is Foreign Policy?   44
Analytical Concepts   48
Definition of Terms   52

PART 2

IV. IDEOLOGY AND OBJECTIVES   57
    Culture, Ideology and Foreign Policy   57
    Ideology: an Individual and Society   61
    Ideas and Politics   63
    Ideological Concepts   63
    Anatomy of a Political Ideology   64
    Ideologies of Foreign and Domestic Policies   69
    The Vision   71
    The Irrational   73
    National Interest   75
    Whose National Interest?   78
    Objectives and Doctrines   79
    Dynamic Character of Basic Concepts   84
    Philosophy of International Relations   87
    Mutual Relation of Concepts   89

 V. FACTORS
    The Role of Factors   94
    Geographic Factor   97
    Economic Factor   103
    Population Factor   108
    The Military Factor   113
    Social-Political Factor   116
    Culture and Social-Psychological Factor   119
    Factor X   124

VI. POLICIES   126
    Strategy and Tactics   126
    Stalin's Strategy   128
    The "Problem Paper" Approach   134
    Alternatives   136
    *Brookings Institution and Development of the
        Alternative Approach*   138
    *Use of Alternatives as Mode of Thinking in
        Politics*   148

PART 3

VII. FORECAST   155
    "Scientism" and Forecast   155
    Functional Theory of International Politics   158
    Alternative Situations   161
    The "Unexpected" Situation   164
    Statesmanship and Foresight   165

VIII. SCYLLA AND CHARYBDIS   167

    Index   175

Introduction

STANISLAS ESTREICHER, Rector of the University of Cracow, my teacher, used to size up books in a few sentences. He argued that a book must have what he called "a wit," a thesis, a description, something more—difficult to be described—but which gave to the book the character and made its sense. If he could not do this with the content of a book he cared little for it. In his opinion, it was lacking "something"—or maybe it was confused. I found in my teaching experience, in university and college courses, that a course must have a purpose, objective sense, its "wit"—similar to books. Stanislas Estreicher died in a German concentration camp in Saxenhausen—a victim of Hitler's foreign policy, which he understood, and the dangers of which he anticipated.

He would certainly ask what this book is about, and expect a few sentences for answer. Firstly, it is an attempt to apply scientific thinking and concepts to foreign policy analysis, though we realize fully the limitations and limits of scientific method in study of human society. Secondly, it is a method of analysis and formulation of foreign policy; it suggests ways of attacking the problem. Foreign policy, in this approach, is viewed as a social process. In this social process three essential concepts are distinguished: 1) ideology—and foreign policy objectives as part and result of the former; 2) factors as elements of power (such as economic, military, population, geographic, and other factors); 3) policies, as courses of action. Policies—courses of action—are determined by elements of power—factors—and released toward certain objectives.

The axis of the study of foreign policy is the study of ideologies (objectives), factors, and policies, as well as their mutual relationship. It may be that my description would be too long for Estreicher's taste. I see him thinking a while and then suggesting, "You wrote a book, prepared a course, on how a foreign policy should be formulated, analyzed, forecasted, not *what* a foreign policy should be today or tomorrow."

I did not try to outline an ideal for foreign policy for peace based on our moral principles, but simply tried to dissect foreign politics as it is actually made, to follow the thought process of those who make it, in order to find some general rules, some general principles of such a process.

Obviously, those who make policy may use different terms for the various elements and the various phenomena I have described here. The making of international politics must not necessarily be a systematic procedure as I outlined. However, whether conscious or not, foreign policy-making, in general, follows the lines which have been outlined here. My modest role was simply to systematize in a certain order a somewhat less methodological process of thinking, in the making of foreign policy.

I would like to stress here that the definitions which were used here might not necessarily fit all social phenomena, as the variety of social phenomena is almost unpredictable. If facts contradict a definition, then obviously, the definition has to be adequately adjusted, or a new term used to define the new phenomena. We need definitions, however, despite their shortcomings, whenever we try to build up an explanatory system or a system of analysis. We have to agree on what we mean by various terms. In the social sciences, however, various terms are often used for the same phenomena, and, vice versa, the same terms for different phenomena. The study of international politics suffers in this respect from the same weakness as do all other social sciences. This issue was discussed more extensively in a special chapter (III—"Semantics and Terminology").

It seems to me that a need is felt for a method of analysis, which would give to a political analyst tools and orientation as to where, from what point, to start the analysis. In a scientific analysis of a foreign policy we shall try, above all, to follow the normal, organized, inductive method from the detail to the general, from part to whole. The analysis may start with long-range objectives. Once we find enough facts and documentation to state, with a degree of security, the long-range objectives of an existing foreign policy, the next step is to analyze the factors one at a time. We try to find how far the factors are in a position to support the objectives and how they have been changed in being adjusted to the objectives. Once we analyze the factors, we can study the policy which was chosen by a given government and how far it has progressed, the time involved, whether the policy or policies are conducive to the long-range, strategic objectives, and what has been the role of short-range, tactical objectives within the whole system. Furthermore, we have to investigate the relationship between foreign and domestic politics of a given country.

In this way, step by step, we can analyze the international politics of a given country. We may also use such a system to formulate a policy by analyzing the factors, policies, and objectives.

In the interest of clarity this approach is advanced from simple or simplified concepts to more complex ones. Concepts developed earlier serve as a frame of reference of the following discussion—the whole edifice is built step by step. A reader, who might be interested in some details in the middle of the book, may have to return to the introductory chapters. However, as concepts are interrelated, they are sometimes introduced in a simplified form before they are discussed in detail. Therefore, the reader may have sometimes an impression of repetition, or inconsistency. For instance, significance of facts in research is stressed before relevance of ideas is introduced. The reader may gain the impression that only facts are relevant in research before his first impressions are corrected in the following pages. Foreign policy is defined in a simplified way, before in a later chapter on terminology the concept is discussed in detail.

Somewhere in the text we repeat this remark, to make the reader aware of the purpose of such presentation.

* * *

Study of international relations throughout all of the nineteenth century was almost limited to study of law, diplomatic history, and later also to geography. At the beginning of this century the study shifted rather toward the field of political science and the term "international relations" appeared in university bulletins. Today this field gravitates toward economics, sociology, too—it becomes a part of a broader area of social sciences. This modest study is a part of the latter trend, especially of this toward integration of social sciences.

Social sciences have been overdepartmentalized. A social phenomenon, a social problem does not emerge so as to fit precisely into disciplines as they were cut. After all, the disciplines are a result, partially at least, of an arbitrary division, determined by necessities of research. The very nature of a problem may, and usually does, need cooperation of several of them. Any international problem is historical, political, economic, sociological; it has its psychological aspects as well as legal. To focus attention solely on one single aspect with disregard of others may, in many cases, give a false picture of the nature of the problem. An integrated, interdisciplinary approach is especially reflected in the concept of factors. Analysis of factors of foreign policy embraces the wide field of social sciences—from economics, political science, through psychology to geography. The concept of national interest, strategic objectives, is also analyzed within a similar frame of reference. Strategic objectives, even the concept of national interest, is not an abstract concept. It is a result of political ideology—the latter is a result of culture and continuously changing social and economic and political conditions. Political ideology, objectives are set that way within a cultural-context.

It is not an accident that countries of a traditionally good, efficient democratic government—Great Britain and the United States—developed what is called "political science" as a part of university curriculum. Similarly, the same countries, in times of growing tensions, pioneer in international relations. In the United States this trend is closely connected with the ideology of the public opinion, college faculties and students as well as that of the makers of foreign policy. It is an ideology of constructive, even organized peace, under rule of law. Those of us who studied in Europe in the twenties and especially in the thirties, remember well the extreme nationalistic spirit which prevailed among students of continental European universities. This spirit contaminated even many professors. The spiritual "climate" of American and British universities was at that time and is today different.

No significant, serious expansionist, nationalist movement has succeeded thus far in the United States. The utmost conservative right wing of the Republican party is isolationist, anti-internationalist, but also anti-expansionist. This is in crass opposition to European rightist nationalist parties which are expansionist, imperialist. American internationalism is Wilsonian—it is an internationalism of mutual-aid and cooperation, not of expansion. Imperialism and colonialism are unpopular generally resented symbols in United States public opinion.

❋   ❋   ❋

The speed of technical change, and, in consequence, social change, had its powerful impact on international relations. Our system of diplomacy, mechanism, of international relations becomes rapidly obsolete. Discovery of atomic weapons has contributed to the great change in distribution of political power. Powers have been divided into atomic and non-atomic. The points of gravity shifted to the former. Two polar centers in international relations emerged, both controlling atomic weapons: a democratic and a totalitarian. The risk of conflict and dangers for Western civilization is great.

Technological and social changes of the twentieth century and emergence of powerful totalitarian systems have made the problems of foreign policy a focal issue. Dehumanization of politics under Hitler, Stalin, and Mao has made a threat of conquest equal to threat of individual slavery, or biological destruction. Sooner or later totalitarian governments move toward aggression and expansion. Democracies have to be alert to any change in politics, any sign of danger. It is hardly possible to evaluate totalitarian foreign policy without a method, without a proper and scientific approach. In times like ours, the study of international relations, study of foreign policy, although still young as a discipline, is becoming a vital part of social science and a vital tool of democracy.

* * *

The future of international relations, future international security, an order under a system of law, is also an area of inquiry. Here past experience is not enough. The past helps to understand our problems today. However, the tempo, speed, of social change, changes in technology create a new situation for which the past can hardly offer an answer. New solutions must be invented, new vision developed—vision for which more is needed than past experience. One time future foreign politics was an area of fanaticism, prophesy and irrational myth-making of symbols: "Third Rome," "Third Reich," or a "Historical Border." In a democracy future international politics is a new frontier of inquiry: a frontier of science, of reason and morals, not one of mythology and fanaticism.

* * *

This study is a result of seven years, although actual writing took only half a year. The concepts were first developed in 1947 in my New York University classes. For several years I used this approach in my seminars at New York University, the University of Virginia and the University of Wyoming. My work in foreign affairs had a counter balance in sociology, in Brooklyn College. The advanced class in method of research in social science of Brooklyn College gave me a chance to clarify my views and later integrate concepts of methods of social sciences with international relations, especially foreign policy. I was fortunate in that I found in this class an unusual group of students. They had abilities, a will to work and study, and a strong interest in the subject. The Brooklyn College student is a very good one—he likes to study, he has serious scholarship, combined with energy and criticism. Interest and criticism of my students have greatly contributed to my work. I also had the privilege of participating in the Brookings Institute Seminars, and this gave me the opportunity to acquaint myself with the "Brookings" or "problem paper" approach, based on alternative policies. There, and on other occasions I exchanged views on problems of methods in foreign policy analysis with the late Dr. Leo Pasvolsky, who combined a sharp and penetrating mind with warmth and friendliness of feeling.

Pasvolsky had a strong interest in application of scientific methods to study of foreign policy. He extended his interest to my work too, which was indeed an encouragement. At the Woodrow Wilson Department of Foreign Affairs of the University of Virginia, where I was invited twice as visiting professor of foreign policy, I met also with interest and encouragement. Professor John Gange and Professor Alfred Fernbach, as well as a group of able students from various parts of the globe, had similar interests. In a seminar, concepts of this study were discussed. Indeed, I greatly enjoyed our work there, especially in 1953 when I shared responsibilities in a seminar on foreign policy with Dr. Fernbach. In the summer of 1953, I presented some of my concepts at the seminar of sociology of international conflicts of Professor Donald R. Taft, at the University of Illinois, where I lectured under the sponsorship of Mid-European Studies Center of the Nat. Comm. for a Free Europe. Professor Taft advanced greatly a sociological approach to international politics, especially to international conflicts. Indeed, it was most refreshing to find there that we were close in our approach to international relations. Those discussions, conferences, seminars, lectures, always gave me encouragement and the comfort that my approach and work were not isolated, but part of a wider effort to develop scientific methods, introduce a broader social science approach to international relations.

I would like to express my thanks to Dean William Gaede of Brooklyn College whose friendly and kindly attitude toward his colleagues is appreciated by all of the faculty. Due to his moral support and assistance the technical chores were taken away from my shoulders. I was given full and most friendly support by Mr. Stetson S. Holmes and Mr. J. B. Hoptner of the Mid-European Studies Center of the Free Europe Committee where I work as a consultant. I am indebted to my colleague, Professor Hugh H. Smythe of Brooklyn College for his interest and attention. He was kind enough to help read the galley proofs and make corrections; his remarks were of great assistance to me. Professor Martin Lean, author of *Sense-Perception and Matter,* read the part of the manuscript on scientific method, causation and terminology. It was to my comfort that Professor Lean, whose major interest is the theory and philosophy of science, found that the manuscript was in agreement with his views and concepts, although he indicated that my terminology might, in certain cases, be different from that used by other authors. I am also indebted to Professor William Attich Reitzel, of Haverford College and the Brookings Institution, for his comments. I am obliged to Philip Zimbardo for reading the manuscript and expressing his opinion from the point of view of an advanced student audience.

Professors Donald Taft and Florian Znaniecki of the University of Illinois read the manuscript and their comments were of great value to me. Prof. Znaniecki's remarks can be found on pages 38 and 93. As the manuscript was already in page proofs, the comments had to be incorporated where space was available although it might have been preferable to use them in a different place.

Thanks go to my wife, Mrs. Priva Gross, for all her cooperation and help, and to my whole family for tolerating my excessive intellectual absence while this book was written over weekends and during my vacation. Miss Elaine Rosen and Miss Dorothy M. Lewenz were kind enough to take on their shoulders the hard technical work in typing the manuscript and arranging for permissions to use quoted materials. Miss Mae Matler prepared the index.

The editor also wishes to acknowledge his indebtedness to those who have generously assisted him in the production of this book, and the following publishers for permission to reprint excerpts from their publications:

Annals of the American Academy of Political and Social Science: "The National Interest—Alone or with Others?" Vol. 282, July 1953, edited by Norman D. Palmer. Excerpts by C. B. Marshall and Norman Thomas. The Brookings Institution: *Major Problems of United States Foreign Policy, 1952–53.* Alternative approach to underdeveloped areas (The International Studies Group of the Brookings Institution) published in 1952; and the *Memorandum on the Lake Forest Seminar,* June 4, 1949. Council on Foreign Relations, New York, 1947: *The Study of International Relations in American Colleges and Universities,* by Grayson Kirk. Dept. of State Publication 2651: *Foreign Policies, Their Formulation and Enforcement* by Ambassador Loy W. Henderson, 1946. Doubleday & Company, Inc.: *The Road to Foreign Policy* by Hugh Gibson. Copyright 1944 by Hugh Gibson. Ginn and Company: *Social Causation,* by Robers M. MacIver. Harcourt, Brace and Company: *The Mind and Society,* by Vilfredo Pareto, 1942, Vol. I. Henry Holt Company: *Democratic Ideals and Reality,* by Halford Mackinder, copyright 1919, 1942. J. B. Lippincott Company: *Fateful Years, 1909–1916,* by Serge Sazanov.

The New Leader: Review of "The Challenge to American Foreign Policy" by John J. McCloy (Harvard University Press, 1953) in the August 3, 1953 issue, by Harry D. Gideonse. National Geographical Society: "The Geographical Pivot of History," from an address by H. J. Mackinder reported in the *National Geographic Magazine* for August, 1904. *New York Herald Tribune:* "Bermuda Conference" by Ned Russell, December 8, 1953. *New York Times:* "Britain Cuts Units Abroad, Build Mobile Force at Home" by Drew Middleton, *The Times,* issue of Jan. 28, 1954; also "The French Crisis, II, Alternatives to European Army Plan are viewed Politically Defective" by Hanson Baldwin, *The Times,* issue of Dec. 25, 1953. *Political Science Quarterly,* "Human Nature in American Thought: Retreat from Reason in the Age of Science," Vol. LXVIII, December 1953, p. 507. The University of Chicago Press: *The Study of War,* by Quincy Wright, 1942. The University of Minnesota Press: "Folkways of Social Science," by Carl O. Sauer in *The Social Sciences at Mid-Century,* published for the Social Sciences Research Center of the Graduate School, 1952. The University of Pennsylvania Press: *Outlines of Russian Culture,* by Paul Miliukov. Ed. by Michael Karpovich, translated by V. Ughet and E. Davis.

FOREIGN POLICY ANALYSIS

PART 1

CHAPTER I

Scientific Approach

The Scope

THE purpose of this study is to outline a method which could be applied to the analysis of foreign policy.

Foreign policy is a system of human actions. It is based on human decisions. Foreign policy is a part of human relations, of social relations. Actions are undertaken by men. Whether they lead to war or to peace—they are man-made. So are the weapons. They are made by men, in order to fight or to defend. Neither weapons nor the geographical conditions foment wars by themselves. Human societies may use certain geographical conditions as much for war as for cooperation. Rivers were avenues of Norman conquest, as they were avenues of medieval trade.

Since foreign policy is a social process, and a result of human actions, we may assume that the general principles of scientific method can be applied to this field similarly as they were applied with greater or lesser success to other areas of social sciences.

The facts and inferences, further—abstractions, generalizations, theory—form the essential elements of an empirical method. In consequence, scientific inductive method, as applied to the study of foreign policy, must also be based on the same elements—on facts and inferences derived from the former, and theories based on inferences.

Can we get facts in a study of foreign policy? Of course we can. In fact, effective foreign policy was always based on

3

good understanding of facts, of realities. We derive our facts in study of foreign policy through observation. Foreign policy in its dynamic aspect is, as was already said, a system of actions of one government towards another, or one state towards another state, or of a government towards an international organization. Those actions and even decisions can be observed and described as facts. However, before such actions are released, foreign policy is a plan, an idea, a doctrine, a system of principles, values, objectives. In short, it is an ideology. Even a simple, purely economic policy, or a policy with such a simple objective as conquest of a foreign territory, is first a plan, an idea, and reflects the culture, values, and objectives of those who make the policy decisions. Foreign policy as an ideology, objectives of a foreign policy can also be discovered, observed—they are facts, too. We can describe such ideologies as we describe religious or magical systems of the American Indians; we can describe actions as we describe beavers, who build a beaver-dam. Once we can describe facts, we can also draw inferences, conclusions from those facts, we can indicate their mutual relationship, we can make abstractions, develop theories. In other words, we have here elementary tools of an inductive, scientific approach.

Of course, there are limitations, and serious limitations, of application of a scientific method to a study of social phenomena. Those limitations are especially strong in the field of social causations, as well as in problems of values and value judgments. With all those limitations, however, scientific method has its application in the field of social relations and foreign policy. Of course, application of scientific method requires an intelligent approach, full understanding of its limitations, but also an understanding of its usefulness.

In foreign policy such a method is used. Real statesmanship consists, after all, of looking at the facts, understanding their meaning, and drawing conclusions from them. This is called realism, in a proper sense. Let us call it "empirical realism." We may draw a distinction between three terms: "empirical realism," "power realism," "opportunism." Realism, as a concept of unrestrained application of force towards the weaker, as an ideological concept belongs to the "principles," values of foreign policy of some—such as Hitler or Stalin. Such a concept of realism, which we may call "power-realism," is different from empirical realism of those who, looking at the facts of the domestic and foreign policy of Adolf Hitler, back in 1939, made correct inferences about his war preparations and dangers. Idealistically-minded labor leaders of Europe were realists when they anticipated war and made inferences from observation of facts—policies of Mussolini and Hitler. Those in Europe and America were realists who anticipated, back in 1943–45, in times of Teheran and Yalta, the expansionist and highly dangerous Soviet policies. Empirical realism should not be confused with opportunism. By opportunism we understand a policy of temporary relief, in violation of fundamental principles, without chances of success in the long run. Chamberlain in 1938 was an opportunist, while Churchill at that time was an empirical realist. Munich —a settlement of 1938, which sacrificed Czechoslovakia as a price of peace, was an opportunistic, but not a realistic, decision. The foreign policy of Col. Beck, in which a Polish semi-dictatorship sided with Nazi Germany against Czechoslovakia, was an opportunistic policy. It was not guided by empirical realism. Empirical realism, in statesmanship, was always based on facts, good logic, good understanding of facts and their mutual relationship. In other words, on elements of scientific thinking.

The first step in a process of good policy formulation, is ascertaining *what is*. In other words, the first step is always establishment of facts as a basis of future conclusions in the direction of *what ought to be done*.

Our purpose is not to suggest *what ought to be done*. It is not the purpose of this book to devise a better, a perfect system of international relations or how to improve the U.N. I am fully in sympathy with such plans and recognise fully an urgent need of our thinking and working in this direction. But this is not the scope of this book. Our primary aim is to suggest methods of observation of the policies of any government in the detached, cool way of an onlooker, to devise methods of selecting and classifying facts of a foreign policy, and to facilitate understanding of their mutual relationship, their meaning.

The concepts of fact, theory, hypothesis—even values— which we shall use in this chapter are closely interconnected; they are not separate, isolated entities. They can be understood; they make sense, only in their mutual interrelationship, in their mutual context.

The patient reader should not expect any startling, new theories. In our discussion of method we shall rather describe the ways "empirical" realists (not opportunists!) have often analyzed international situations, probably without being conscious of and without specific interest toward problems of methods. This discussion, then, will be chiefly, if not solely, an exposition of methods by which policies can be analyzed and formulated.

The Role of a Hypothesis

Scientific inquiry does not operate with concepts of absolute truth. Our theories are only stronger or weaker hypotheses, our description of facts—especially in social sciences—are short of precision and perfection. Any new theory which, through verification, indicates that a former theory was false, takes the place of the former. Science advances through continuous testing of theories. New facts, unknown before, may change entirely our hypothesis, which was based on a deficient, or incomplete body of facts. The scientific approach is then a dynamic approach, in which theories, even facts are continuously tested. Error is not a sin in a scientific approach. In fact, a contingency for error is accepted as a rule, as part of scientific approach. Paradoxical as it may sound, error is a part of scientific inquiry. One of the purposes of inquiry is the elimination of error, which is persistently present, to an extent that contingency for error becomes part and parcel of scientific equipment. Science, to an extent, is a system of hypotheses.

Distinction between a working hypothesis and findings, or conclusions, is relevant. A working hypothesis is a general idea, a "guess," an assumption, based often on some insufficient knowledge of facts—we may even say, on fragments of facts. Claude Bernard, one of the founders of experimental medicine, calls the working hypothesis "idea *a priori*." A working hypothesis is usually based on some, though insufficient, experience. The working hypothesis becomes in research a guiding idea which is tested against the facts—a sufficient body of facts. A stage of higher approximation to veracity is reached once the working hypothesis is verified by facts or relationship between facts. We call the result of such operation a conclusion, inference or finding. A working hypothesis, tested by experimentation, or precise observations, is accepted as certainty for as long as it is not destroyed by new theories, verified by facts, or by new facts. In a scientific inquiry, however, a conclusion is usually a stronger, better verified hypothesis; it is not an absolute.

A hypothesis is, in consequence, a flexible tool of an inquiry. A hypothesis can be changed any time during the research, as a consequence of discovery of new facts which necessitate such a change. New facts may indicate an error in the hypothesis, or its entire falsity. But the same facts which have killed the working hypothesis may again become a basis for a formulation of a new working hypothesis or reformulation of the old.

Hypothesis and axiom are two different concepts. Axiom is applied in deductive inquiries while a hypothesis is a concept of an inductive inquiry. An axiom is a general proposition, accepted at the beginning of an inquiry with the understanding that it cannot be changed during the whole logical process. An axiom is a stiff proposition. In an inquiry based on axiom, the whole logical edifice is based on the former; therefore a change of axiom during the operation would simply destroy the latter. Axioms are used in mathematics. A proposition, that through a point over a line one can draw only one parallel is an axiom. In Euclidean mathematics we may use this axiom—but then, we have to stick to this assumption during the whole operation. In an empirical study, based on inductive reasoning, we use hypotheses. The very conception of causality however can be regarded as axiomatic.

The field of foreign relations is a field of humanities and therefore it might be appropriate to make the distinction between dogma and hypothesis, scientific and dogmatic thinking. An axiom is a voluntarily accepted proposition as a premise of a logical process. The axiom might be abandoned by the mathematician; he may also try a logical operation based on an entirely different assumption. This was done *e.g.* by Lobatschevski, Bolyai and Rieman who established a non-Euclidean system, based on different assumptions. A dogma is a proposition of religious character. An authority may be established to comment upon the dogma. A thinker, writer, or student, however, is not permitted to change the dogma or to question it. Once he questions the dogma, he puts himself outside the religious group, or he is ousted by the religious group. In politics we have many examples of dogmatic thinking. Galileo argued that water will rise in a pump to a certain altitude, but it cannot rise higher because it would break of its own weight. This was a hypothesis. This hypothesis, as Conant[1] brilliantly described it, was subject to inquiry of Galileo's two able students—Torricelli and Viviani. They found that Galileo's hypothesis was false. Air pressure determines the altitude of water, as well as of mercury in a tube. They changed, destroyed Galileo's hypothesis—there was nothing wrong in their action. They acted according to the principles of scientific inquiry. They destroyed a *hypothesis*, not a *dogma*. Some of Galileo's scientific theories, however, put him in a controversy with what was at that time a virtual Church *dogma*. In religion dogma is a legitimate part of faith. Science, however, has no place for dogma. In empirical, inductive thinking a hypothesis is applied; in deductive thinking, an axiom might be used. Religion and science are different areas of human experience. They operate within different value systems. Thought processes in those areas are different. These systems are not contradictory. Religion, the area in

[1] James B. Conant, *On Understanding Science*, Mentor Books, New York, 1951, p. 41.

which non-scientific values are so strongly expressed, is in another, different area of our experience.

Now, we may try to apply these scientific concepts to our efforts—to the analysis of foreign policy. Scientific inquiry is based on facts and abstractions. In the analysis of foreign policy, facts, well described and verified, form the basis of inferences. Usually, however, a general, cursory knowledge of certain facts forms a basis of a working hypothesis. A visit to Germany, back in 1934, daily reading of "Angriff" and "Völkische Beobachter," observation of a general mood was sufficient to form a hypothesis, a working hypothesis that Hitler and his government were preparing for war. Occupation of Tibet by the Chinese Communists might be a sufficient basis for a hypothesis that Mao's objective—one of the objectives—is a Communist rule in India. We may call a working hypothesis such statements—based only on rudimentary, general knowledge of facts. We may also call such a statement, a statement on *a level of a hypothesis*. Now, we may use this hypothesis to gather more facts. We found facts about German re-armament, propaganda, fifth column activities. We found activities of the Indian Communist party, penetration of communist agents into the bordering Indian provinces, and other facts. Careful gathering of this intelligence, their evaluation—analysis of factors, policies, and objectives—may or may not support our hypotheses. In our case, the hypothesis is, I think, valid. Once the hypothesis has been supported by careful analysis of facts, we may reach an inference of a higher level of verity; we may call such a level a *level of finding* or *level of conclusion*. Our level of findings is a better, stronger hypothesis. We may have difficulty in finding a sufficient body of facts to verify our hypothesis, at the moment when policy is made. Usually, a fuller verification of hypothesis, a more conclusive confirmation, has to wait until documents are published, or problems solved one way or another. Diplomacy and documents are still to a great extent secret. However, Hitler's objectives of expansion could be anticipated very early. Though they were verified by the very expansion which came later, it was not difficult to anticipate such a policy years before, or at least in the times of Munich. There was no need for full verification—the hypothesis was strong. It seems to me, that usually we have enough facts to identify a given policy. Looking at Soviet policy in Europe and Asia we may correlate the facts and relatively securely identify the goals. Of course, it is hardly possible to get Stalin's original statement made in closed, secret meetings. We may get them in years to come. But present actions are sufficient for formulation of a hypothesis. On November 5, 1937, Adolf Hitler presented to his General Staff a plan of conquest of Europe. Today we have documents of this meeting, 386-PS presented by the prosecutor to the International Tribunal in Nurenberg.[2] At that time, in 1937, we had sufficient facts, without document 386-PS to formulate a hypothesis of such a plan. The documentation is a part of verification— a posteriori—after the war. It would be hardly possible to get such a document before. But was it necessary for our hypothesis? Not at all. If we had this plan, no hypothesis would be necessary. In the formulation of hypotheses, as in all scientific thought processes, essential is the ability to relate facts.

Neither axiom nor dogma has an application in a sociological research, nor do they have any in foreign policy analysis. Hypothesis concerning the purpose of a given policy can always be changed by discovery of new facts. In a totalitarian government, a kind of dogma or quasi-dogma is set by the "Führer," "Vozd" or whatever is the symbol for the leader. Torricelli and Viviani could defy a hypothesis of their master Galileo, could destroy it, indicate that his hypothesis was false. Who would have the courage in the Soviet foreign office to advance a hypothesis that Stalin's theory is utterly false? Galileo used a hypothesis; Stalin, a dogma.

Selection of Facts

An important element of foreign policy analysis is, of course, facts. The number of facts is, from a practical view-

[2] See John W. Wheeler-Bennet, *Munich, Prologue to Tragedy*, Duell, Sloane, and Pearce, New York, 1948, p. 11.

point, unlimited. Therefore, selection of facts in a research is of primary significance. How do we select facts?

Bronislaw Malinowski, the anthropologist, was an unusually trained and talented observer. He had full mastery of fact finding, fact gathering techniques. His *Scientific Theory of Culture*,[2a] published posthumously, was probably his most mature theoretical work, a definitive presentation of his theory. The prominent observer and fact gatherer states that one cannot start to collect facts without a certain theory, without a certain general idea. In other words, even our working hypothesis has a theoretical frame. We have to have some purpose to collect data. We may change the purpose of research and the general idea which has helped to formulate the hypothesis, but still we have to start with something. Selection of facts is usually directed towards a certain purpose. Alfred North Whitehead explains that "observation is classification." Classification requires a certain theory, certain abstractions, in short, principle of division—*principium divisionis*.[3] In any scientific inquiry facts do not suffice. We have to have facts and various types of abstractions, facts and theory.

Let us take an example. Let us imagine we are analyzing Mao's foreign policy. We shall try to discover facts concerning the degree of Mao's dependency upon Moscow; Mao's hand and influence in Indo-China; Mao's plans in Asia; his military establishment; and, of course, a number of other factors. We may analyze step by step: first, Mao's policy in Korea. We may try to find out whether he is playing an independent role, or whether he is entirely a stooge of the Kremlin. It would be of importance to find out whether there is a rift between Mao and the Kremlin. In each case, however,

[2a] B. Malinowski, *A Scientific Theory of Culture and other Essays*, with a preface by Huntington Cairns. University of North Carolina Press, 1946, p. 7.

[3] Max Black regards classification as "the sorting of things into classes," and proposes that: the classification be made clear at each stage (the differentiae be clearly described), the division be exhaustive at each stage, and that each class be divided into non-overlapping subclasses. Max Black, *Critical Thinking*, New York, Prentice-Hall, Inc., 1952, pp. 216–218.

in each example, we shall try to discover facts, pertaining to
our hypothesis—in other words, we shall select facts. This
selection will be guided by a general hypothesis, which in
turn we formulated on the basis of our general knowledge of
the social sciences and political science, as well as of our
specific knowledge of communist theory, Mao's history, and
on a body of previous experience.

In this large mass of facts we have to establish a "hierarchy
of importance." Some facts are of minor significance, the
others of primary. Which are more significant than the others?
There is no general answer to it. Proper selection of facts is
the test of craftsmanship and intelligence. So is intelligence
and wisdom in understanding of mutual relationship between
facts. Proper selection of problems, facts and methods is, after
all, a test of scholarship. In Germany of the twenties a lunatic
fringe of nationalists used to meet in small groups in inns,
drink beer and talk nonsense. From one of those meetings of
beer drinkers grew the Nazi movement. Of course, it did not
grow as an isolated phenomenon. Social, political conditions,
psychological manipulations and a number of other factors
have contributed to its success. However, there were few observers who attached significance to those meetings and nonsense talk. Few would believe at that time that those men
who met there would be instrumental in the extermination
of probably more than eight million innocent victims, including hundreds of thousands of children. Few would pay
any attention to their publication—to their tiny *"Blätter."*
Still, those meetings and poorly edited papers were more significant than many headlines. What will happen with the
Soviet Union after the collapse of communism? Already today
plans, doctrines, ideas are discussed in a number of obscure,
small publications, read by a handful of theoreticians and
leaders. Still, those ideas, or some of them, might or might
not be important.

Those two interdependent principles, selection of facts and
hierarchy of importance, as instrumental as they are in any
inquiry, harbour dangers of grave, while even unintended
error. We select facts on the basis of a certain general idea,

not yet verified by facts. Furthermore, we apply a selective process in choosing significant facts. Such an approach leads easily to a preference we may give, consciously or unconsciously, to the selection of such facts as prove our thesis. In other words, we are never free of certain values, views, intentions. Our working hypothesis, our general idea we start with, is not free of values.

There is also another aspect of this ambivalent problem. As much as we have to realize such dangers, values are not necessarily an impediment in the discovery of truth; they might even be helpful as vital stimulus, without which no inquiry moves. When the democrats of Europe and European labor leaders were warning that Adolf Hitler's policy would lead to war, of course, they were also antitotalitarian, and their interests in Hitler, Nazism and peace were determined by their values. When they advanced the hypothesis that Hitler prepared for war, their values were present. When Churchill warned about Nazism and Hitler and advanced his hypothesis that Hitler meant war, of course he was interested as a European, Englishman, and antitotalitarian, in the dangers of Nazism to Europe, Great Britain and democratic traditions. However, the fact remains that, in spite of their strong values, those men correctly anticipated the Nazi foreign policy. Similarly, the keenest analysts of Soviet foreign policy were anti-Stalinists, strongly anti-communist. Men like William H. Chamberlain, Dallin, Abramovich, Nikolayevsky, and so many others, who contributed to the "New Leader" magazine in New York, anticipated Stalin's policy correctly. The editor of the paper, Sol Levitas, and its editorial policy were always strongly anti-communist. Anticipations of those men of strong values were correct. There was passion in their work, perseverance in their effort. Some other weeklies of liberal character in New York tried hard to be objective, detached, cool. Some of their editors made an effort to apply as much detachment and objectivity as they could to study of Soviet policy. Some historians followed a similar line. In 1945, because of the general desire of American public opinion to end wars forever, because of the growing popularity of the United Nations, the pessimists, who warned about Stalin's intentions were not popular. The optimists did not like them—accused them of bias, partiality. Those men of strong values were correct in their anticipations, while those who emphasized their objectivity, detachment, were deficient in their analysis. Some of them were awakened, once Stalin took over Czechoslovakia—some were not. Values may not necessarily result in a wishful thinking. Intelligent analysts with definite, even strong values, with abilities of observation, endowed with what we called empirical realism, might sometimes be better students of foreign relations than those who lack any definite convictions.

The danger of error in the process of selection of facts, however, is always present. In the social sciences, we may easily, almost always find facts and authorities to prove our points. The British historian Macaulay wrote in his *Essay on History* that we may put together a number of true facts and give a false picture. One who would describe Hitler's "Autobahnen," Olympic games, schools and "Kraft durch Freude" while omitting facts about concentration camps, abolition of civil rights, war preparation, would give us certainly an entirely wrong impression of the Nazi system. How to apply properly our concepts of hypothesis and selection? Already Bacon, in *Novum Organum* (XXV, XLVI), emphasized that many try to prove their points by gathering the affirmatives, facts which confirm a chosen point. Bacon advised to pay the same attention to the affirmatives and negatives—facts which confirm our point as much as those which negate its validity. Claude Bernard suggests even that a good researcher should above all pay attention to facts which deny the hypothesis.

We may apply this principle to our study of foreign policy. In selection of facts, we are guided by our hypothesis. However, we should as carefully consider facts which contradict our hypothesis as those which confirm it. A most careful evaluation of both will lead to rejection of some facts as irrelevant, and retention of others as relevant. In this choice we have to be guided by experience, intelligence, wisdom— our knowledge of history, political science, social sciences in general. This choice between "affirmatives" and "negatives" is not a matter of simple balance or "golden middle road." One set of facts was Stalin's statements about his peaceful intentions towards the West and Eastern Europe, his assurances to Mr. Beneš, Mikolajczyk, and all the others, that it was not his intention to intrude into domestic problems of Eastern Europe; the other set of facts was the penetration of the communist apparatus into the administration of the East European republics, manipulations of communists through which they got control of strategic points. On one hand, there were assurances and learned articles, that Mao's Chinese communists are only agrarian reformers; on the other, hard facts about communists' strategy and tactics, communist objectives and ideology. Truth is not in between—as truth is never a compromise between a big lie and true facts. When an analyst was selecting facts, those which supported the hypothesis about communist expansionist objectives in China and those which contradicted it, it was not his task to choose a few from each. The task was to select those which were relevant, which fit into the general trend of development, facts mutually related, which clarified—and not obscured—understanding of the whole situation. A proper selection required experience and understanding of the significance of those facts. It is not enough just to describe facts, collect them and throw on a heap of factual material.

Science is constructed of facts as a house is erected of stones, wrote Poincaré in "Science and Hypothesis." However, he rightly taught that accumulation of facts is not science, as a heap of stones is not a house. Relationship of facts is essential. This relationship usually has to be understood before all the facts are gathered. Understanding of relationship requires an idea, an abstraction, a theory, without which science does not exist. Facts are fundamental. They become, however, fruitful only when combined with an idea. Understanding of few facts is much more valuable than knowledge of many without understanding them. The former is a test of intelligence and scholarship; the latter is useless. And furthermore, a relevant question is always, "What kind of facts," not,

"How many." Facts which contribute to our understanding of phenomena are important, not facts which are useless, as a library of old telephone directories—a collection of facts without any connection and interrelationship.

Values and Facts

A problem to which hardly a satisfactory answer can be given in the social sciences is the problem of values and research. In social sciences values, as a rule, accompany our research. We have our views, biases, likes, and dislikes. As much as we control them, still they may influence our choice of facts and they definitely influence our choice of problems. Choice of problem in social sciences has almost always a value behind it. Values of course influence the quality of "objective truth" through our subjective attitudes and values.

In defense of the scientific method in social science, we may argue that values are present in any research. Karl Mannheim in *Ideology and Utopia* traces ideas, theories, doctrines, to the interests and purposes of social groups. Relation between ideas and societies which produce them is the frame of reference of sociology of knowledge. Scientific ideas grow only in societies where scientific interest has been developed, where value was placed on a search for truth, on freedom of research, and status given to those who professionally devote their lives to scientific inquiry. Scientific ideas grow in a society which has values, not in a vacuum. Directly or indirectly, values influence any research. Early nuclear physicists, passionately interested in splitting an atom, had a definite interest, even bias, in their belief that such an experiment was both possible and significant. The values were present in their choice of problems. For the sake of truth let us stress the difference between social science and physics in this respect. A physicist can verify his theory much more precisely than a social scientist, as he can isolate his variables, his facts, he can use quantitative methods more successfully, his observation and experimentation are a very advanced proposition. In other words, the research stage, the process of verification, permits in the natural sciences as a rule, and especially in physics, the separation of values from facts. In the social sciences, separation of fact and value is a much more difficult, if sometimes at all possible, proposition. Furthermore, choice of objectives in foreign policy— indeed, any problem-solving approach—needs a value. Objectives in a decision-making or problem-solving process as a rule require a value ("right" and "wrong").[4]

It might be advisable to summarize in a few sentences this never-ending discussion. In a problem-solving approach in our study of foreign policy, and generally in social sciences, values are present. Our concept of national interest contains a value judgement. The concept of national independence, freedom, as much as concepts of power, profit, and economic advantages, are human values. Choice of objectives contains those values. Our interests in definite areas, issues of foreign policy, contain elements of value. Our choice of facts and even description of facts might be determined by values. Values might be present in the natural sciences, in a choice of problem. But for all practical assumptions of research, we may postulate that a physicist, in a problem-solving approach (splitting of atom) has to deal with facts—the social scientist with facts and values. This does not mean, however, that objectivity in a research stage—in a stage "what is," not in a stage "what to do"—is a lost virtue in social sciences and in consequence in study of foreign policy. The British government, back in 1939, decided to defend Poland in case of Nazi attack. The German government decided to attack Poland. The German Foreign Office and general staff, preparing for such attack, had to evaluate Polish military forces, Polish economic potentialities to support an adequate defense, moral force of Poles to resist, and many other factors. They had to evaluate those factors as objectively and as carefully as possible, to make their conquest successful. Underestimation of Polish strength might have defeated their purposes; over-estimation would result in unnecessary expenditure of their

[4] For more extensive discussion of this issue see Feliks Gross, "Limite de los Valores Cientificos en la Investigacion Social," *Revista Mexicana De Sociologia*, Vol. XV, Mai–Aug. 1953.

potential. They had to be "objective" in order to be successful. The British foreign office and military leaders had to make a probably very similar inquiry in order to evaluate chances, needs, and timing of Polish defense. It may be that the results of the inquiry were identical—while the objectives of the British and of the Germans were entirely different. Objectives of both governments contained values. In the research stage, however, of an existing, empirical situation, values were probably under control. An extreme view, an argument that presence of values makes an empirical observation and proper evaluation of facts of politics impossible, is erroneous. Values are present, but they can be restrained; they must not necessarily deprive us of our objectivity. On the other hand, they supply the necessary stimulus, vigor of our inquiry. As was mentioned already, their role is ambivalent. They form also one of the limitations in our research and discovery of "objective" truth. There are unfortunately more of those limitations present in scientific inquiry. In the process of observation and experimentation, the limitations of our own senses are another limitation of discovery of the "objective truth," and a very important one.

For the sake of terminology in foreign policy we may indicate here that objectives in foreign policy might be both means and values. As final, strategic objectives, ends, or long-range goals, such as "Greater Germany," they are values. Short-range objectives, tactical objectives, such as the German-Polish treaty of 1934 as a step of Nazi policy toward disruption of collective security, are means toward a farther value-goal, in our case, Greater Germany. One may argue, however, that this means contains a value.

Operational Method and Method of Analysis

The usual empirical procedure we shall call "operational method": beginnings of an actual research with formulation of a working hypothesis, selecting facts as a second stage, and conclusion as third stage. In the conclusion, relationship between the facts is eventually established. The term "method" may be applied to another concept, which we shall call the "method of analysis."

Science requires both facts and theory. There is no theory without facts; facts without theory are useless. A theoretical equipment is a necessary collection of tools for fact gatherers. Without theory, fact finding cannot be purposeful. The theory, through its method of analysis, provides a general idea, concepts for a formulation of a working hypothesis. The "method of analysis" is a part of theory. It is an application and procedure of application of theory, of general idea, of concepts, to a concrete formulation of a hypothesis which, in turn, is part of an operational method. In social sciences such theories as historical materialism, geographical determinism, or poly-causal, pluralistic (multiple causal) approach are examples of theories with corresponding methods of analysis. Similarly in psychology, the behaviorist school has one corresponding method of analysis, the Freudians another.

The method of analysis guides the working hypothesis while the working hypothesis guides a concrete, definite research. The method of analysis sets the direction which may decide operation of the working hypothesis in selection and hierarchy of facts. The working hypothesis is an important part of a derrick called the operational method, which is digging for facts. The method of analysis indicates the field of research, the "segment." The method of operation searches in the narrowed field for answer. The method of analysis narrows down the area; the working hypothesis gives a focus to research in this narrowed area. The bacteriological method of analysis indicated the area of research in the struggle against the bubonic plague. The area was—the world of germs, bacteria. The working hypothesis gave focus to an assumption that the rat is the carrier. Through change of hypothesis fleas and lice have been identified as true carriers. Should the "method of analysis" contain falsities, then of course the working hypothesis will contain such falsities. The theory is incomplete if it emphasizes only certain factors, neglecting others. In such a case the working hypothesis will be incomplete, too, and selection of facts will be accordingly slanted, unless the researcher is on guard against a one-sided selection of facts, against stretching facts to his hypothesis.

Theory

Theory which is a product of ideas, requires more than a simple, even crude empirical process. Development of theory is rooted on one hand in facts, and on the other in vision, imagination, talent of such, in qualities which are close to art. Neither science nor the scientific process is limited to crude, empirical operation. Ideas, vision, imagination continuously open new vistas, new avenues of inquiry, of interest. On the other hand, the facts continuously test those broad hypotheses, conceived through vision and imagination. If the facts contradict the theory—facts carefully selected—then, of course, the theory must be changed. The theory is chained to facts. Moreover there is a continuous interaction and interdependence of facts and theory. The results of research return to theory, which is a well-organized storeroom, where the results of our research are placed on proper shelves, and plugged into proper outlets, which connect them with other, related findings. Without vision and imagination theory, however, would lack the spirit, the soul of scientific inquiry. Few men of science contribute new ideas. Indeed, this requires great talent, great spiritual qualities, and often a fortunate accident, which may lead to such an idea. Many, however, may learn proper techniques of research, proper application of the operational method.

In a scientific approach, we shall use a system, a theory, if it can be used to discover relationship between facts in a given situation or in a given reality. A communist, who operates with a quasi-dogma, not with a hypothesis, will try to squeeze the facts so that they fit the theory.

Theory, the method of analysis, is a tool. If it does not work, we have simply to drop it and select another one. A handyman would be foolish to use a hammer instead of a monkey wrench. In social sciences, however, such foolish things are often done.

Method-Centered and Problem-Centered Approach

The method, then, is subordinated to problem, and not the problem subordinated to method. In a method-centered approach, we select as problems of our research and interest, problems which fit our method. Hence solely such problems are selected to which our method can be applied. Important problems, to which a given method cannot be applied, are left outside research activity. This trend is apparent today in sociology, above all by uncritical enthusiasts of the quantitative method. Problems which are not subject to a research with application of measurement, are regarded by those researchers as outside the area of "true" sociological research. In a problem-centered approach, the method is adjusted to the problem. If a method or a theory cannot be applied, if a theory contradicts the reality and the method hardly can help in fact-finding, then of course we have to look for different tools, as was already said. Study of foreign policy concerns vital problems, problems which concern us directly. In a scientific approach to foreign policy analysis, we are not interested in method, for method's sake. The method of analysis as much as methods of operation, are useful only if they help to understand the meaning and consequences of a foreign policy which we observe, if it helps to formulate policies or policy objectives, and in consequence helps to make intelligent choices and intelligent decisions. Similarly, from the point of view of education, of study of international relations, only such an approach is sensible. A detached method-centered approach might be legitimate only in an inquiry concerning solely methods, and devoted to the perfection of methods. A dogmatic, method-centered approach to foreign affairs study, however, might be detrimental. We shall return to this problem in our final chapter: "Scylla and Charybdis."

CHAPTER II

Causation

Foreign Policy as a Social Process

FOREIGN POLICY might be initiated by a decision of a government. Once, however, a decision is made, its enforcement releases social processes. Roughly three types of processes might be distinguished: cooperation, conflict, neutrality or coexistence; the latter based on limited cooperation, avoidance of conflict. It is well known to sociologists that we may have mixed processes—cooperation and conflict, and even strong conflict or intensive cooperation may be accompanied by some of the opposing processes. Even during a war—an extreme form of conflict—there is some cooperation, for instance in transmission of mail and food parcels to the war prisoners through the Red Cross. Types of social processes are recognized rather through emphasis and gradation, emphasis on types of interaction and intensity of the process. Any of those actions, of course, affect states and governments, but they also affect individuals and groups.

Foreign policy of a government is not an isolated phenomenon. It is simultaneously a doctrine and a system of actions, and it can be understood within the context of other governmental activities: the objectives a government has chosen, its ideology, the economic situations, political conditions, a general culture of a nation (culture in an anthropological sense), psychological attitudes, emotional tensions, geographical situation, and certainly other factors; in a word, within a context situation. Each case has to be studied on its own merits within the "context situation" as related to concrete conditions. When Hitler and his party chose a foreign policy of conquest, there were a number of factors present, which permitted Hitler to develop such a policy. The almost psychopathic emotional reaction of large parts of the German population, the psychological and ideological factors, gave him popular support for such action. Military traditions and military establishment gave him an instrument of such policy. Economic conditions and system of Germany gave him arguments to convince business leaders who had a definite interest in their support of Nazis. Furthermore, Hitler himself is a product of a certain culture (in an anthropological sense), of certain sociological conditions and ideological influences. Hitler, Goebbels, Göring and others were products of certain social processes, which already existed when they were born. Ludendorff and those similar to him were there when the former were children. The latter, too, were products of social processes, result of actions of men, groups, societies. The relationship in other words is a functional one. To understand a foreign policy, we have to consider this whole complex picture, the "context situation." In other words, we have to observe a given foreign policy as a part of social process, a very complex one. Many factors—which we may call here variables—are present in such a process: economic, political, ideological, psychological, geographical and others—which we shall try to discuss in a specific and more systematic way in a special chapter (Part II. Chapter V. FACTORS). Some of those variables are more stable—as, geography; some, more dynamic. The variables are in a constant interaction, and constant change. In consequence, application of a scientific method is difficult. In fact, the complexity of the problem, the number of variables, their interaction, is numerous and complex to such extent that some of the leading scholars in the field of international relations doubt whether scientific method can be applied in this field. The whole field of international relations is even questioned as a discipline. Professor Grayson L. Kirk in his *Study of International Relations in American Colleges and Universities* (Council on Foreign Relations, New York, 1947) indicates that the field of international relations (if such a discipline can be developed) "covers almost every field of social sciences." "This brief survey of the field of international relations," writes Kirk (p. 21) "cannot but impress one with its exasperating complexity." There is strength in Kirk's point. The difficulties of foreign policy study and analysis can hardly be minimized. The limitations of methods are a consequence of the very character of the problems, of the very qualities of the whole field of international relations.

With all its difficulties of scientific approach, the field of international relations and foreign policy became of vital significance in our times. Realizing the difficulties, we have to try to do our best within those limits. The field of foreign relations is not the only one. In the whole area of social sciences, mutual interrelation of all disciplines is more and more apparent. Specialization—with all its merits—does not give a full answer any more to problems of scientific research. Specialization meets its objectives if it is integrated within the whole system of social sciences.

The realization of the shortcomings of narrow specialization without integration is reflected today in our educational trends. Courses in integrated social sciences are introduced today in American colleges. Experimentation with such courses on an introductory level is quite extensive. Efforts are made to integrate into one social science course, sociology, psychology, economics, political science, and sometimes also philosophy. In that way, a general, integrated approach to social problems is presented to the students. It is hard to judge today what will be the success of this interesting experiment in education. One of its purposes is to deal with the multiplicity and complexity of social processes— the very problem which we face in study of foreign relations.

The integrated social science approach represents a trend toward functional integration of social sciences. Another effort to integrate social sciences is reflected in area-approach. A geographic area of cultural, economic, political, historical and geographical homogeneity is chosen such as North Africa, North America, South East Asia or similar ones. Various fields of social sciences are applied to such an area for a better understanding of its social and political problems and its significance in world politics. Area approach is not contradictory, in fact, it is complementary to the functional integration of social sciences. An area specialist is both a specialist and a generalist. An East European area specialist, or a Central America area specialist applies in fact an integrated social science approach to the vast field of the problems within a given, geographically limited area. Of course, both of those approaches, functional integration and area integration, have their shortcomings. Necessarily, the approach may lack the depth and understanding of detail. Again, under the circumstances we have to work within the limits of those shortcomings. The marginal fields of disciplines, difficult as they are, are fruitful and challenging.

Study of foreign policy by both functional integration and area integration may offer a partial answer to questions raised by Dr. Kirk. Such an approach also offers equipment for a study of foreign policy as a social process, not as an isolated government decision.

Conflict and Cooperation

Some theories interpret foreign policy as a part of a complex social process. Marx looked upon it as a part of the whole development of a capitalistic system, the result of the economic forces and their dialectics. Not only the foreign policy, but its results, the consequences of a foreign policy, form together a complex of interacting social forces. Professor Donald R. Taft in his *Preliminary Introduction to the Sociology of International Conflict* (mimeo, Aug., 1950, Urbana, Ill.) advances a hypothesis that international conflict may tentatively be viewed as the intersection (so to speak) of complex dynamic multilateral social processes, which are essentially understandable, if difficult to understand, and that the cooperation of all disciplines is needed for their comprehension and possible control.

According to Taft, war may be explained in terms of relationships between some six aspects of the development of national states.

a. Social evolution which produced the value systems found in each state. No two are alike, but all would have been alike had social relations been identical. No people are then "to blame" for their culture.

b. The nature of the values characteristic of each national culture. With reference to war these are "dangerous" when either of two types: (1) those inherently, logically or emotionally leading to conflict; (2) those not of that nature but hindering understanding.

c. The nature of the structure of each national culture society. Here the relationship between sub-group and classes is very important. It is the integration of the influence of these sub-groups which explains national policies.

d. Leadership, which may appear as extraneous to the culture if leaders have had wide contacts with other cultures. Yet leaders are all products as well as powers.

e. Current situations as they play upon the "national character" so produced. War is on the whole more situational than cultural though both influences enter in.

f. Conflicts of interests. This is really not an additional influence, but a type of situation.

Taft's approach recognizes fully multiplicity of variables. While Marx's approach is largely monocausal, Taft's approach is an example of complexity of international problems. Taft copes with this problem on a broad, integrated level, crossing lines established artificially by faculties and departments.

Similarly, international cooperation is a much more complex process, than is often realized. Many of us, in our younger years, believed that once an institution—like the League of Nations—is created, cooperation between the governments would be a matter of course. We have learned the hard way that institutions of international cooperation do not suffice. A government in power, which participates in an international institution, must meet other conditions, to release a true cooperation. The government, its members, parties in power must have an interest and will to cooperate for peace, cooperation must be one of its foreign policy objectives. The government, the parties involved must share a certain minimum set of common values with other governments or parties. Without common values cooperation is not possible. Certain techniques must be established. If those conditions are met, then an international institution like the League or the United Nations becomes a working instrument of cooperation toward the goals set by the charters. Italy under Mussolini, the fascist government, participated in the work of the League. The same government started war against Abyssinia. Mussolini's government had different objectives from the League. Neither his government nor he himself had a will to eliminate war as an element of national policy. The League of Nations could not, at that time, produce by itself an effective cooperation between Fascist Italy and Abyssinia. The process of cooperation was and is more complex; a charter by itself, important as it is, cannot create a desired pattern of behavior. The institution is a machinery; to work it needs will, common objectives, interests, values.[5]

Social Causation

Foreign policy is a study of social processes, a study of dynamic, changing situations, in which variables, facts, are mutually interrelated.

Already a hypothesis anticipates such an interrelationship which is either causal or functional; a hypothesis anticipates an answer as to how things happened, what happened, what are the objectives of a policy, or simply anticipates mutual interrelationship, interdependence of variables. The first is usually causal, the second functional. In consequence, a hypothesis or conclusion is usually a causal or functional assumption. Both in a causal and in a functional approach, the significance of facts and variables lies in their mutual relationship, in their meaningful connection.

The choice of facts, based on a working hypothesis, contains already the elements of this relationship. We observe and choose facts which are causally or functionally related.

[5] For more extensive discussion, see: Feliks Gross, "A Sociological Theory of International Cooperation," *Calcutta Review*, Vol. 127, May, 1953.

Facts mutually related are relevant, significant in hierarchy of importance. By such a relationship we can *understand* a given, observed foreign policy—how it is made, and, maybe, why it is made, what are its objectives. The causal or functional relationship of facts or variables is the core of theory and of the method of analysis as well as of the working hypothesis. Both concepts are essential in the method of analysis and of operation on the level of a working hypothesis, and on the level of findings.

We may begin our discussion of causation with examples of causal theories in international relations. For the sake of clarity, at the expense of subtlety, we shall overemphasize those examples; we may even present them in a crude and rough way. With this in mind, we may suggest that Marx's or rather dogmatic Marxist thesis of foreign policy is based solely on economic causation. The contradictions of the capitalist system are the cause of imperialism. *Ergo*—Stalin and Molotov and communist tutti quanti interpreted in a distorted application of Marx's theory French and British struggle against Nazi Germany as imperialistic war of the West against Germany. This was the official propaganda and party line back in 1939–1941. This line was repeated by Communist party leaders all over the world. In such a theoretical approach, arbitrarily chosen economic factors in Great Britain and France were suggested as cause; war, which Hitler started in 1939, was presented as effect of this economic factor. In a deterministic, geographical approach, geographical position of a state is the main, or the only factor of its policy. Mackinder, in his early theories, back in 1904, argued that the geographical position of Russia determines its foreign policy. Whether a Tsarist or revolutionary government, he argued, the policy of a government which will control the territories of Russia will be the same, as geography determines the direction of its policies. In a crude interpretation of geopolitical theories, the geographic situation determines the expansion of a great power. Geographic position is the cause; foreign policy, the effect. German nationalists were prone to interpret their eastward expansion as a result of their "mission" and geographical position. In a theoretical approach, which emphasizes the ideological variable, ideology is responsible for the conduct of foreign policy. Fascism was the cause, in such explanation; war in Abyssinia, annexation of Albania, effects. In Hans Morgenthau's theory a drive for power is the cause of conduct of foreign affairs.

TABLE I

A Simplified Scheme of Causation

C_1, C_2, C_3 = C = causes
E = effects
N = causal nexus

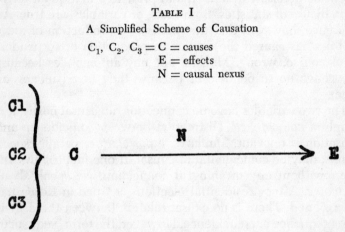

An error can be committed when: 1) C or E are not true, or 2) C and E, though properly described and true, are arbitrarily chosen, and coincidental. In the latter case the error is committed in evaluation of the inference, *causal nexus* (N).

In all those examples of a causal approach, three items can be distinguished: cause, effect, and connection between both. We may call this connection causal nexus. Causes—in a "simplicist" approach—are conditions, complexes of facts, variables from which other facts result. The latter are called effects. G. H. Mead in *Philosophy of the Present* calls causation a relation of an event to conditions under which it occurs. In both concepts, a relationship between cause and effect is implied. Error in theory, in method of analysis, hypothesis is possible a.) in the description of facts—cause, effects—or b.) in the inference—causal nexus. The facts might be untrue, or wrongly selected, slanted. Then, of course, the inference, based on false premises, will be false. The facts might, however, be well and precisely described. They might, however, be arbitrarily chosen, with no relationship between them.

The facts may be well described with no meaningful connection, without a logical nexus. We call such an assumption coincidence. Statistics may certainly indicate increase in the production of automobiles in the U.S. since, say, 1905, and decrease in the use of suspenders by men. Both trends might be precisely described and presented in a quantitative way, by use of statistics. Both facts, or variables, are true. An inference, however, that the increase of production of automobiles has caused the decline in production of suspenders is, of course, wrong. Men do not buy automobiles because they have no suspenders or because they saved money on them.

The two variables have no connection, no causal nexus; it is simply a *coincidence*. Distinction between coincidence and causation is relevant. Similarly, a *correlation*, parallel social trends, may be coincidental or causal. If one fact follows another without any meaningful connection, we speak about *sequence*. After presidential elections, a truce in Korea has been signed. There is no causal relation between these. It is just a sequence or coincidence. However, the term "sequence" is most often used as a concept of a rhythmical periodic repetition of certain facts which have no meaningful connection—such as opening of schools in September and New Year's celebration. To sum up, the following concepts have been defined: *causal nexus, coincidence, sequence, causal correlation*, and *coincidental correlation*.

Now we may return to our examples. A communist propagandist might have described the unemployment in Britain in the thirties as cause, entrance of Britain into the war in 1939 as effect. Britain's war was according to theory an "imperialistic war" in search of markets, raw materials. Both facts, unemployment and war, are true and may be properly described. But there is no causal nexus. The error in this explanation is in the logical or causal nexus. Precise description of facts might be impressive, convincing, may give the impression of truth. However, an analysis of such interpretation should point to error in relationship of facts, in causal nexus. The two facts, two variables, are simply not causal.

Britain's government entered this war because of a number of different implications: its very existence and survival were at stake; because of a political, economic, social threat to the nation; because of vital dangers to the Empire.

Monocausal and Pluralistic Approaches

We may call *monocausal,* or *monistic,* schools which believe that there is one main cause of foreign policies, a cause present in all countries and all cases. The key in a monocausal approach is a "prime-mover" of foreign policy, such as economics, geography, or others. In a polycausal, or pluralistic approach, we postulate multiple causation, presence of more than one causal motor, more than one variable. Monocausal approach is to an extent an *a priori* approach, as we accept here one causal factor in operation, before exploring the situation; moreover, we eliminate the possibility of causal factors other than this one, as we accept a priori economics, or geography, or any other one as *the* cause. Monistic approach is usually a deterministic one.

Professor Quincy Wright in his basic study, *A Study of War* analyzes causality of wars. Wright analyzed the causes of six major wars: Moslem Conquests, Crusades, Hundred Years' War, Thirty Years' War, The French Revolution and Napoleonic Wars, World War I. Reviewing opinions on the causes of war, Quincy Wright concludes: "War has political, technological, juro-ideological, socio-religious and psycho-economic causes." Wright's is far from a monistic, monocausal explanation of war; he represents a pluralistic viewpoint.[6]

[6] Quincy Wright, *The Study of War,* University of Chicago Press, 1942, pp. 717–743. Analyzing opinions on causes of war Wright mentions: ". . . belligerents are powers which became involved in war in the process of organizing political and material forces in ever larger areas, that they are states which became involved in war to realize more complete legal and ideological unity, that they are nations which became involved in war in the effort to augment the influence of particular political, social, and religious symbols, and that they are peoples which became involved in war through behaving according to prevailing psychological and economic patterns."

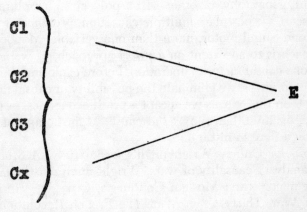

TABLE II

Monocausal Approach

C ———————————————— E

One cause (C) responsible for Effect (E)—foreign policy.

Multicausal or Pluralistic Approach

C1
C2
C3
Cx

E

A number of causes (C_1, C_2, C_3, . . . C_x) responsible for effect (E)—foreign policy.

We may, however, also look at monocausal schools, or theories, in a somewhat different way. Borrowing Pareto's approach (*Mind and Society*, New York, 1942, p. 33), a given, even monocausal theory may interpret a part of a situation, while another theory may explain another part of a given situation. To repeat—an economic factor is a powerful motor of foreign policy. It accounts for many foreign policies, or parts of it. There are also many possible economic interpretations of a foreign policy. Some may account for one situation, or part of it; others for another situation. It might be hardly possible to find one economic causal theory which would explain *all* foreign policies and *all* its parts. At best we could say that probably in all foreign policies the economic factor is present.

A theory might be true, entirely false, or it might be not necessarily erroneous, but it may not apply to a given situation. The same is true with some other monocausal theories, for instance certain geographical theories. A study of British policy in China would certainly indicate the decisive significance of the powerful economic factor as a cause of British policy. Was the economic cause equally strong in the formulation of American foreign policy toward Poland in President Wilson's 14 points? Were the *identical* economic causes responsible for the policy of rulers of Austria, Germany and Russia toward Poland, which culminated in partition, as they were in Wilsonian policy of self-determination of nations? Of course, the economic factor was a powerful cause in the United States foreign policy towards Europe, after World War II. However, economic causation, connected with problems of destruction and reconstruction of Europe, was here entirely different from the economic causes responsible for the Opium War in China one hundred years ago. According to a Leninist interpretation of United States foreign policy, one should expect that, after the Second World War, the United States would try to destroy European industry, expand onto the European Continent, to secure markets for itself. Destruction of European industry would eliminate the most vital industrial competitor of America. Instead, the United States government is spending millions in order to put European industry on a competitive level, to modernize, improve it, to create large markets, raise standards of living. According to the Leninist stereotype, the United States government should support a division of Europe, to prevent integration and modernization of European industry. Instead, the United States government supports enthusiastically the Schuman plan, and plans for European integration, as a condition of European economic recovery, while the Soviet government favors division and pulverization of Europe. Of course there are economic causes in the United States foreign policy toward Europe; however, they are different from Leninist theory. The Communist, and extreme one track mind Marxist, as all orthodox doctrinaires, look for one type of economic cause in all historical events. The truth is different from their scriptures. There is no one, sole type of causation, but there are many types, many forms, a large diversity of economic causation. It cannot be established *a priori* for all cases. Every single case has to be explored, and types of causation have to be discovered for every single case. Similarly, in every case various causal factors, such as economic, ideological, geographic and others, have to be identified.

Ideology and values were often underestimated as causal variables in the study of foreign policy. It seems to me that even the economic factor is to a large extent an ideological and cultural one. After all, the concept of profit is a value, accumulation of money is a value, and a desire, characteristic for our culture, but not for all cultures; attitude toward money and business is a cultural attitude. Of course human motivation is determined by biological needs, but it is also determined by cultural values, even by irrational elements which we hardly understand, and which hardly fit a scientific framework. Nazi foreign policy objectives and ideology called rather for a psychiatrist, not solely for an economist.

Scholars like old-day alchemists are in search of one miraculous idea, a "golden mono-idea"—one theory which would explain everything. Maybe it exists, maybe not. The essential empirical device is to use our theories within the context of a real, existing, empirical situation. Without such a present, existing situation, we may project ourselves into a future international situation, based at least partially on past experience; reconstruct a past situation; or construct an imaginary situation. To borrow some concepts from Karl Pearson's *Grammar of Science*, we may in such cases postulate what is "probable" but not what is necessarily "provable." The same accounts for broad generalizations. Important as they are, they pertain to the "probable" which, in a context situation, in a concrete situation, may or may not be "provable."

Functional-Interactional Approach

How significant were the various causal factors? Here, we cannot give a precise answer. In social sciences we cannot isolate variables. We cannot isolate the psychological factor from the economic and evaluate it quantitatively. In physics, we can isolate a single variable and discover a cause-effect relationship, which can be precisely identified. We can select one variable—for instance, heat—and discover that metal, when heated, will expand. We answer a question as to how things happen, and single out a variable. In social sciences, and hence in a study of foreign policy, such an isolation of variables is hardly possible; the variables, or causes, appear in mutual interrelationship; they are mutually interacting.

The interdependence of variables is so extensive that it might be difficult, sometimes impossible, to distinguish the cause from the effect. Difficulties in isolation of variables, complexity of their mutual interaction, impose another limitation in application of scientific method in certain problems of the study of foreign policy. In sociology Vilfredo Pareto tried to cope with this problem, by elimination of the concept of causality, and by introduction of the concept of function. According to Pareto, we can discover mutual interdependence, maybe interaction of variables. Discovery of mutual interdependence we may call function (interaction). Pareto writes about the common error "which lies in substituting of cause and effect for relationship of interdependence."[7] He introduces the concept of function and variables instead of cause and effects. Variables are the changing social processes—function indicates their mutual interdependence. In a causal approach one variable is identified as the cause, the other as effect. Concepts of functional interaction were successfully applied by sociologist-historians such as R. H. Tawney in his *Religion and Rise of Capitalism* and to an extent by Max Weber in his *Studies of Capitalism and Protes-*

[7] Vilfredo Pareto, *The Mind and Society,* Harcourt, Brace and Company, New York, 1942, Vol. I., p. 255. For digest of Pareto's concept of function, see Pitrim Sorokin, *Contemporary Sociological Theories,* Harper and Brothers, 1928, pp. 422 ff.

tant Ethics. Although Weber emphasized the ideological factor in the study of capitalism and Protestantism, Tawney, following the path of Weber, indicated rather the mutual interdependence, mutual interaction of both variables, than a cause-effect relationship. In a monocausal economic approach, rise of capitalism would be regarded as cause of change in religion. Both change in economics and change in religion have influenced each other, according to Tawney's presentation.

The burden of the battle in defense and place of the concept of causation in social sciences has been taken by Robert M. MacIver. MacIver's position is that in all our conscious activity—in doing, or thinking—operates some concept of causation. The concept of causation, according to MacIver, is a result of our experience; it is not an a priori concept; it is an inference which we make out of experience which we had, living in environment. "Deny the concept of cause, and every other concept—succession, change, continuity, time itself—vanishes into thin air."[8]

Without causation we could hardly analyze any situation, hardly suggest a policy. How could we explain Czechoslovakian partition without a causal approach? There must be causes which resulted in the downfall of this prosperous democracy. Hitler's foreign policy, his aggression, is certainly one of the fundamental causal factors. In a functional approach it would be difficult to find a practical answer. We would have to find Czechoslovakia's government's actions as almost equally responsible for its downfall. Experience, facts, teach us it was not so. Pareto could dispose of the concept of causation as he was not interested in practical problems and solutions. He wrote, "the great enemy of social sciences: the mania for achieving some practical result." But in study of foreign policy, we are definitely interested in practical solutions. Objectives, factors, policies, are elements of our causal relationship; and concepts of causality permit us to understand what is happening, and how, and choose policies—they answer the question, "what should be done."

8 Robert M. MacIver, *Social Causation*, Ginn and Co., 1942, p. 5. Used by permission of the publishers.

The concept of function finds a wider application in the field of theory, on a higher level of abstraction. It seems that the concept of function might be re-interpreted in a causal sense, and I would side with such a causal-functional interpretation.

Mutual interdependence, or functional-interaction, usually means reciprocal, mutual causation of such quality that it is hard or even impossible to distinguish causes from effects. *Whenever it is impossible to discover clear causation, the concept of functional interdependence is appropriate.* Social interaction, mutual influence of variables is a general phenomenon, and the concept of function, inter-action, is applied in sociology. We may use then, in our study of foreign policy, concepts both of causation and function inter-action as complementary concepts.

To use again Pareto's approach, or, rather, to paraphrase it, the latter concept (function) may interpret parts of a situation, or certain situations—where the former (causation) is not applicable. Interestingly enough, Pareto in his later work returned to the concept of causality, though he qualified this concept.[8a]

Alternative Effects

In physics the same cause, isolated from other variables, produces the same effects. Heat will always expand the metal. We shall be able to discover precisely *how* things have happened. In social sciences, the same variable may produce a number of alternative effects. The same Gospel produced the Inquisition and Torquemada in Spain and St. Francis of Assisi in Italy. The same New Testament has resulted in Protestantism in Anglo-American countries and in Catholicism in others. The variable, a causal factor as we already know, cannot be isolated from other causal factors, which are different in different historical and geographical situations,

---

[8a] "L'étude de ce qu'on appelle de *causes*, si par la on entend des faits en certains rapports avec d'autres, appartient à la science et rentre dans la catégorie précédente des uniformités. Mais ce que l'on appelle les *causes premières*, est en général toutes les entités qui dépassent les bornes de l'éxperience, se trouvent par là même en dehors du domaine de la science." Vilfredo Pareto, *Les Systèmes Socialistes*, Paris, 1925.

in different societies. Our observed variables, once put into operation in a given society, are immediately in an interaction with others. The constitution of a Latin-American country might be a copy of the United States Constitution. However, as it operates in a different society, in interaction with different causal factors, it produces different effects. Universal military service was introduced in Switzerland as early as the XIIIth century. It became in Switzerland an important factor in the development of Swiss democracy. Compulsory military service introduced in Prussia in the XIIIth century later became a vehicle of despotism and totalitarianism. Similarly, a foreign policy applied toward or by a given country might result in different effects than the same applied by or toward another. British policy of "appeasement" which might have been effective, for instance, toward democratic France, was utterly ineffective toward Nazi Germany.

Our cursory discussion of social causation, as applied to study of foreign policy, makes us further aware of limitations, shortcomings in application of scientific method to such study. These limitations indeed have to be realized continuously.*

---

* We may return here again to the problem of integration of social sciences. Professor Florian Znaniecki emphasizes rather the specialization than the integration of social sciences. He sees the need for integration on the level of practical problems.

Commenting on this chapter, Professor Znaniecki wrote: "Specialization of 'social' or, more generally, 'cultural' sciences is necessary, because each deals with a different category of phenomena. Their integration is indispensable only when *practical* problems are concerned; for the solution of a practical cultural problem requires the cooperation of specialists in several branches of theoretic knowledge. The same applied to natural sciences: e.g., the solution of practical problems in the realm of agriculture requires the cooperation of biologists, chemists, geographers, and physicists."

Professor Znaniecki's comments arrived after the book was already set in page proofs, therefore, they had to be put where space was available. His remarks pertained above all to page 24 and following.

CHAPTER III

Semantics and Terminology

The Meaning of Words in Foreign Policy

A PRECISE use of terms is relevant in any systematic study and application of scientific method in research. However, for centuries the field of foreign policy was an area of human activity in which words were used to conceal, rather than to express actions. Words uttered by diplomats meant something different from those uttered by other mortals in everyday life.

In some diplomatic negotiations terms were used, as well as statements, which were almost metaphysical. Still, such statements percolated sometimes into history books, and were accepted by some at their face value. Statements, concepts were accepted, without further analysis, without being questioned any further. In tsarist times a Russian diplomat may have stated—and this was stated often—"the Russian people, or the Russian nation, desires to achieve its century-old ambition—the access to warm waters." What does this mean? It was a "social myth" of a certain social class, of a certain social stratum of Russia of the nobility, bureaucracy, army officers. If, however, in times of the Crimean War, one would ask a Russian serf around Tula and Kaluga whether he felt the historical urge toward warm waters and Constantinople, he would probably make a sign of the Holy Cross, look at you with bewilderment, and without understanding a word of this statement. Pressure toward Constantinople was a policy of the Russian government—tsarist and later Communist; it was a policy which might have had support of a part of a ruling class whether feudal, in tsarist times, or communist bureaucracy today. The Russian nation as a whole, however, was never consulted on this issue. *Raison d'état*, "historical mission" and *tutti quanti* were accepted without further discussion, as long as behind the empty phraseology were sharp bayonets and adequate firepower. It is not too proper to partition a country for the sake of expansion, in violation of treaties and promises. Even the most amoral politician tries to justify his action on moral grounds. Metaphysical phraseology and platitudes then come in very handy. High-sounding words form a smokescreen for brutal violence. A simple question, directed to those who use undefined or metaphysical symbols in foreign policy, "What do you mean by that," might have been not only embarrassing for those who used them, but also beneficial for clarification of issues.

Language is an important tool of science. Through language we express our thoughts. Application of scientific methods requires a careful selection and use of terms, a proper agreement on content of various word-symbols.

The metaphysical platitudes are not the only instances of confusion. With best intentions symbols are used for a word content, which misguides even the person who is using such a term. The term "nation" is often used in an anthropomorphic sense. Instead of speaking about the foreign policy of the Soviet government, we speak about the foreign policy of Russia. When the French government accepts or rejects a proposition, we say "France accepted or rejected a proposition." Governments may or may not represent the majority of a nation. The American, British, French, and Swiss governments technically do; the Soviet and Spanish governments do not. Governments, which decide about foreign policies, are not necessarily representative of nations. The use of terms "France," "Great Britain," "Russia," "Spain," instead of "governments of France, Great Britain, Russia, and Spain" makes the four countries appear in our speech as four persons of similar qualities. The complex decision-making process is replaced by anthropomorphic concept of individual decisions. Differences of forms of government, differences of the whole "modus operandi" are soon forgotten. Foreign policy looks in such context like a game between four or five persons.

Sometimes the structure, symbolism of a language, or even an accepted parlance forces on us a certain mode of expression. It is impossible to specify every time in a discussion that by "France" is understood the French government supported by a parliamentary majority; the parliament elected in a certain way, as well as those voters who support the majority, while the others may have opposed it. In this book as well it was hardly possible to change certain expressions, though we prefer to use a more precise denotation to specify the government of a country.

Furthermore, the same symbols sometimes have different meanings. Well-trained diplomats, precise in their use of words, may incur difficulties. Parties may use words which have different meaning in each language, or terms which are defined differently by both parties. They may argue because of the use of terms. Change of terminology or clarification of terms may bring an agreement. Problems of order and procedure may fall into this category. The term "control" has a different meaning in English and in German, Russian, Polish, or French. In the latter it means "supervision." Some languages may have concepts, terms which cannot even be translated into other languages. Bronislaw Malinowski[9] mentions the following German words as untranslatable into English: *Sehnsucht, Weltschmerz, Schlachtfest, Blutwurst, Grobheit, Gemüt, Gemeinheit*; French: *liaison, au mieux, belles lettres*. Words referring to moral and personal values change their meaning in various languages, he argues; compare the Spanish, French, and English symbols for honor. "English," he writes, "changes east of Suez; it becomes a different language in India, Malaya, and South Africa." May I add that many languages lack a single term for "policy," though they have a term for "politics." In Polish, one can only describe the term "policy" by "political action."

The English spoken by students at Brooklyn College consists of the same sounds as English spoken by students of the University of Virginia. Still, the same utterances may how-

[9] B. Malinowski, *Coral Gardens and their Magic*, American Book Company, New York, 1935, Vol. II, p. 12.

ever, have a different meaning. A statement made by students on the grounds of University of Virginia, regarded by their colleagues and faculty as a strong one, may be regarded by students on the campus of Brooklyn College as a mild one. While a student at the University of Virginia is used to understatements, the Brooklyn College student is not afraid to use a superlative. Even within the same country utterances may have a different meaning.

Modern linguistics and cultural anthropology, the general field of semantics, have already made considerable contributions in this field. The significance of this problem is recognized today in the field of international relations. The Foreign Service Institute, of the Department of State, published the brilliant linguistic essay of B. L. Whorf.[10] Whorf discusses problems of the Hopi language. He indicates that culture and thoughtways of the Hopi Indians of the North American Southwest have been formed by the kind of language they have developed. It may seem at a glance that this subject is remote from the art of diplomacy. The contrary is true. Whorf's study indicates that a language has to be considered in a cultural context (*mutatis mutandis*—a similar thesis was advanced before by Ogden, Richards, Malinowski, Sapir and others). In negotiating and dealing with foreign governments, the culture in which the members have been raised, the culture of the nation they represent, is closely connected with the meaning of the words they use in their negotiations. The meaning of their words can be properly understood only within such cultural context.

We may fully realize the need for adequate definitions and precise use of symbols in foreign policy research and study, and still find such a task not only difficult, but in certain instances impossible.

Social problems are different from phenomena studied in physics. In physics, in natural sciences, concepts can be de-

[10] Benjamin Lee Whorf, *Four Articles on Metalinguistics*, Washington, D.C., 1950. This publication contains the following articles: 1. Science and Linguistics; 2. Linguistics as an Exact Science; 3. Languages and Logic; 4. The Relation of Habitual Thought and Behavior to Language.

fined and described almost always in a precise way. The difficulties in proper defining can be overcome by what Bridgman calls "operational" definitions, which describe how things are done, how they are produced, or how they work.[11] In our study of foreign policies, we may sometimes use operational definitions which should not be confused with our concept of "operational method." It is, for instance, very difficult to define such phenomena as Nazi penetration into Czechoslovakia or Communist penetration into democratic governments. The operation, however, can be described. We may apply an operational definition.

Some social concepts, I should say even social phenomena, are of such a nature, however, that they also escape operational definition. How to define a "nation"—the Swiss, without a Swiss language and the French who have a national language fall into the same category. Still, both are nations. There are many definitions of a nation, but the phenomenon is of such variability that it is hard to give a precise, all-embracing definition. In fact, cultural variability is the essential characteristic of and difference between various nations (cultures). Still, in spite of difficulties in defining, nations do exist as social realities, and, vice versa, definitions cannot create nations.

This example indicates another, reverse side of the same problem of terminology and definition. Important as the latter are, they require an exercise of moderation and balance. It is easy to lean to the other side, to switch from one extreme—misuse of symbols, confusion in their use—to another one, to a peevishly pedantic doctrinaire, even to a virtual obsession. An obsession with problems of proper terminology and semantics may limit our abilities of expression, our freedom in using words and phrases, when we deal with broad, vast, essential problems. It may create obsessions,

[11] P. W. Bridgman in *Logic of Modern Physics,* Macmillan Co., New York, 1928, credits Einstein for operational character of concepts. Before, many concepts of physics were defined in terms of their properties. In the new approach "concept is synonymous with the corresponding set of operations." For instance, we define length by describing operations by which length is measured.

which cripple our vision and imagination, this irreplaceable and rare quality, essential both in a scientific approach as well as in approach to problems which, by their nature, greatness, and imminence, may escape the formulas and narrow methods of scientific exploration of human society and its less regular, rhythmical and more irrational expressions. Therefore, the efforts for proper, precise use of terms should be kept within the limits of needs and possibilities. The problem of terminology as so many others has an ambivalence of its own.

What Is Foreign Policy?

Granted the limitations of terminology and definitions, granted on the other hand also the need of precise terminology, we shall proceed now to our next assignment: definition of foreign policy. No method of analysis can be advanced without proper terminology and definitions.

We may keep in mind our limitations: what was already said about metaphysical use of words, confusion of meanings, difference in meaning of symbols in various cultures and languages, relationship between language and culture, difficulties of precise definitions in certain instances in social sciences, and even the possible shortcomings of an obsession, overemphasis on precise definition of terms.

The same symbol, we argued, may have a different meaning, different content for various persons, or in various cultures. The same is true with the term "foreign policy." It even has a different meaning for two men, prominent in the field of diplomacy, at the same time and in the same country: Ambassador Hugh Gibson and Ambassador Loy W. Henderson. Gibson in his penetrating book *The Road to Foreign Policy* (Doubleday Doran, New York, 1944) seems to argue that the United States has no definite foreign policy. Henderson, to the contrary, is persuaded in his "Foreign Policies, their Formulation and Enforcement" (Dept. of State, 1946) that the United States has a definite foreign policy.

Ambassador Gibson's argument was at the time, that the United States had no definite, "real" foreign policy (op. cit.

p. 145). He entitled a chapter in his book "Why We Need a Foreign Policy." Foreign policy, according to Gibson, means planning. Government must plan; even a grocery store does, he argues. A government must have a plan of the conduct of foreign relations, a plan prepared and approved on the highest level.

Foreign policy is a continuous process, requiring continuous study of changing situations, re-interpretation of the plans. Such a policymaking has to have a counterpart in an alert and competent diplomacy. According to the changing situation, the diplomats, within the general frame of the plan, should have more freedom of action. Gibson* defines foreign policy as:

> . . . a well rounded, comprehensive plan, based on knowledge and experience, for conducting the business of government with the rest of the world. It is aimed at promoting and protecting the interests of the nation. This calls for a clear understanding of what those interests are and how far we can hope to go with the means at our disposal. Anything less than this falls short of being a national foreign policy. (p. 9)

Henderson argues to the contrary that the United States has a definite foreign policy. Quotation from his "Foreign Policies, their Formulation and Enforcement" (pp. 2–3) clarifies his point: †

> The charge is frequently made that the Government of the United States has no foreign policies; that we are drifting somewhat aimlessly in an uncharted new world to an unknown destination; that the State Department flounders in the presence of each new problem and attempts to solve it without seriously considering how the solution might affect the broader interests of the United States or how it might impair our ability to meet fresh problems of the future. I want to assure you that we do have well-established foreign policies. *We have long-term foreign policies which are as stable and as permanent as the traditions and way of life of the American people. We are also con-*

* From: *The Road to Foreign Policy*, by Hugh Gibson. Copyright 1944 by Hugh Gibson, reprinted by permission of Doubleday & Company, Inc.

† Department of State Publication 2651.

stantly formulating shorter-term policies in order to meet the ever-shifting world situation [my italics]. These shorter-term policies, in order to be effective, must always lie within the framework of our long-term policies and must reflect the desires, aspirations, and hopes of the American people.

How are our foreign policies formulated? So many factors are involved that I would not venture to undertake a full discussion of them. I shall, however, touch briefly on some of them.

Our long-term basic foreign policies are molded by tradition. Just as our common law is the heritage of centuries of experience in the field of human relations, so our basic foreign policies have gradually taken form as a result of a series of decisions of an international significance which began even before the Declaration of Independence of the United States. Some of these decisions are to be found in public statements made by those responsible for the conduct of our foreign affairs.

There has not been a President or Secretary of State of the United States who has not left an imprint of some character on our foreign policies. Each succeeding administration makes decisions to meet the particular needs of the times and these decisions become interwoven into foreign policy traditions.

Many decisions which still influence present foreign policy were contained in communications to foreign governments, others in communications or memoranda addressed to the President or to other officials of this Government.

Finally, the Brookings Institution's research staff defines the foreign policy of a nation as:

a complex and dynamic political course, that a nation follows in relation to other states. The foreign policy of a nation is more than the sum total of its foreign policies, for it also includes its commitments, the current forms of its interests and objectives, and principles of right conduct that it professes.

(*Major Problems of United States Foreign Policy*, 1952–1953, the Brookings Institution, Washington, p. 375). A careful distinction is made between "a foreign policy of a nation" and "a nation's foreign policies," which we shall discuss later.

Gibson's definition is based on concepts of planning and foresight. He is concerned with the mechanism in the making of foreign policy. Gibson outlines a vigorous proposition of what a foreign policy ought to be. His ideas are progressive and imaginative. Indeed, the making of foreign policy today requires careful planning and decision on the highest level. On the other hand, this is hardly possible without freedom of action on a diplomatic level, within the limits of a decision. Proper research is a prerequisite of intelligent decision. Moreover, foreign policy ought to be a continuous process based on foresight and research.

Henderson, to the contrary, is not concerned with the question of what a foreign policy ought to be. He tells what it is at present and outlines a rather conservative picture. Accumulation of doctrines, traditions and previous decisions forms the foreign policy of the United States, says Henderson. The Brookings Institution research staff gives a broad, general definition which would embrace both concepts, while Gibson and Henderson use the same term for somewhat different concepts.

Do all nations or only certain nations undertake actions which we call "foreign policy?" This, of course, depends upon how we define "foreign policy." Gibson's definition would require a well planned, continuous action. As much as Gibson's point is convincing in this matter to this writer, as much as we may agree on the necessity of what Gibson may call "real" or "definite" foreign policy, still we need a broader, I should say more empirical, operational definition for our purpose; for a method of analysis.

Every government has some kind of relations with the governments of the neighboring countries. Even two states, located on one island, such as Santo Domingo and Haiti, have some kind of relations. Their governments have to choose a certain course of action, or instruct officials to refrain from certain actions. Practically every government today, through the United Nations, has some kind of relations with others, and every government has to decide on a certain pattern of behavior, certain courses of action, or refraining from action toward other governments. This is indeed what we call foreign policy. A decision to have no relations with another country, to have "no definite foreign policy" is also a foreign policy.

Analytical Concepts

Adolf A. Berle, Jr.'s brilliant essay *Natural Selection of Political Forces* (Kansas University Press, 1950) is an attempt at a synthesis of political science. Political action, political force, according to Berle, requires two elements: ideology and an organizational set-up, an "apparatus." "A political force," says Berle, "consists of a centrally attractive idea surrounded by an organizational apparatus" (p. 22). Ideologies such as democracy, socialism, and nationalism are translated into action by an "organizational apparatus"; i.e., political parties.

Foreign policy is a political force, too. The apparatus is the whole governmental set-up: foreign office, diplomacy, military and naval establishment; more—the whole organizational network of the state. Foreign policy is also the whole system or course of actions (policies) toward another government, governments or international body. The actions (policies) of this government concern the state and its problems. But foreign policy is also a doctrine, a system of principles, objectives, traditions, concepts, such as the concept of national interests, "raison d'état." In short, foreign policy is also what we may call an ideology. Strategic objectives, an important element of analysis, are located in ideology. A foreign policy as an ideology might oscillate from a carefully elaborated system to just a rudimentary concept of objectives, rooted in an idea of national interest, as an idea of survival, or continuation of a definite form of government. Factors are material and non-material conditions of foreign policy. Industrial capacity is a factor; so is the geographic location of a country, cultural pattern, political institutions, military preparedness, historical traditions. The ideology of foreign policy also plays a role as a factor. For practical purposes of analysis, however, it has to be separated. Objectives of foreign policy cannot be achieved unless factors are adjusted to the goals. In consequence, in a rational approach (which is not the only approach in politics, which in many groups is an irrational proposition) objectives are determined by factors.

Objectives, policies and factors are mutually interdependent, they are functional and interactional. We separate them for the sake of inductive method, but we have to realize continuously, that they are mutually interwoven, that the concepts are even in certain instances overlapping. The inductive procedure which is applied here advances from specific to general. Complex and general problems, situations, have to be dissected into smaller particles as our foreign policy concepts were. Thus, smaller elements can be better understood, and the mutual interrelationship of facts or variables can be more easily discovered that way. Descartes' third principle in his method pertains precisely to this device. "The third (principle) is, conduct my thinking in an order, starting with objects which are most simple, most easy to understand (to know), in order to advance little by little, as by degrees, to the understanding (knowledge) of more complex (composées). (*Discours de la méthode*).

A distinction has to be made between a wider field of international relations, and a narrower foreign policy as a part of the former. The field of international relations embraces all types of complex activities and relations between nation-states and nation-cultures, both an area of inter-political and inter-cultural (inter-societal) relations. Here belongs the study of differences in national cultures, tensions, between nations, national-cultural attitudes toward other nations, inter-cultural relations, diffusion of cultures through specialized agencies, international norms of conduct, and other similar studies. Study of foreign policy is concerned with inter-political (inter-state) relations. However, results of study and research in international relations as "factors" have a wide application in foreign policy analysis and formulation. In other words the focus of interest in study of foreign policy is on inter-political relations. This division is of course purely technical (one may even say, artificial), justified by specialized research interest and practical needs.

The problem of relationship between study of foreign policy and international law is of particular interest. Relation between both disciplines is close to the relation between law and sociology. The rules and customs of international conduct, form the avenues of courses of action; they also set the limits and restraints of conduct of foreign policies. International organizations form the mechanism through which the actions—foreign policies—operate, and which form the moving force of those mechanisms. The field of international law is an important field in study of foreign politics, but, of course, it does not overlap the study. Its elements can be found in ideology, principles and pattern of conduct.

Foreign policy is both an ideology and a complex, dynamic system of actions of one government toward other government, governments, political groups or international bodies, in order to achieve certain objectives. We call the course of actions, policies. Objectives are part of ideology (strategic objectives) or parts of means (tactical objectives). In an analytical approach, choice of objectives is determined by factors (general conditions and elements of power). Study of foreign policy is as well a study of ideologies and actions concerning international politics of other political groups and organizations, other than governments, or inter-governmental bodies, particularly of political parties. Relations and actions of governments involve the whole organizational network of state, and also potentialities and inhabitants of the state. Therefore relations between governments are transformed into relations between states; i.e., inter-state, inter-political relations.

A careful distinction must be made between "foreign *policy*" and "foreign *policies*." By foreign *policy* we understand a phenomenon and a study already defined. Maybe the term foreign *politics* would permit us better to emphasize the semantical difference with *policies*, courses of action. Practically, almost the same symbol is used here (policy and policies) for the whole complex concept, as defined, and for courses of action or a single course of action, the latter being only an element, a part of the former. However, such is the usage of the terms, and introduction of new terms might be in this case rather confusing. Therefore, we prefer to follow the Brookings Institution's terminology, and indicate the differences between the concept foreign *policy* and foreign *policies*.

The study, the science, or, maybe better, the discipline of foreign policy is in consequence a study of: 1. ideologies and objectives, 2. factors, 3. policies. Similarly, these three concepts are essential elements in the formulation of a hypothesis and discovery of causation, in a concrete situation. The working hypothesis is based on a general evaluation of factors, policies, objectives. Interrelationship of those concepts serves our causal or functional explanation. Conclusion in consequence is based on verification of the hypothesis—verification of assumptions concerning ideologies—objectives, factors and policies. Working hypothesis about Hitler's strategic objectives in times of Munich could be based on evaluation of his ideology, as presented in "Mein Kampf" and other Nazi publications; change of factors, such as change in production toward armaments, psychological mobilization, increase in military potential and others; policies, such as Nazi policy of penetration into East European countries, previous policies toward the Austrian Republic; all those policies related, their sequences, gave a picture of their purpose. We may discover a causal or functional relationship among all three concepts or between objectives and factors, objectives and policies. Objectives in an operational approach, are causes, change of factors and policies effects.

Operationally, conquest of Europe was Hitler's objective and *cause* of his economic military, psychological preparations. The latter were changes of factors, *effects* of the former.

While we discuss any of the three elements, whether ideologies, factors, or policies, the key to their understanding in a foreign policy study is in their continuous mutual interrelationship. Therefore, we had to digest first in a brief presentation the basic concepts, before we advance with their more detailed discussion. This may be responsible for certain repetitions, which could not be avoided, except at the expense of clarity and at the expense of the very approach which emphasizes the mutual relationship.

Definition of Terms

Terminology of foreign policy has been defined by the research staff of the Brookings Institution.[12] Establishment of a precise terminology, as the former one, is an important contribution toward development of scientific method of analysis. The Brookings staff gives also its critical evaluation to limitations of terminology. Difficulties of definition, overlapping of concepts are realized, and the reader is made aware of them. In the Brookings terminology the term "ideology" is not applied. However, "national interest," "objectives," "principles," even "commitments" are part of the concept which we have called ideology. The terms of Brookings Institution are applied in their publications and studies. On the whole, we follow this terminology in our discussion. Besides the terms, defined by the Brookings Institution, however, a number of other concepts were defined and discussed throughout this book.

Terms

(Excerpt from *Major Problems of United States Foreign Policy* 1953–54) Brookings Institution, Washington, pp. 373–6, prepared by the International Studies Group.)

The terms *national interests, objectives, policies, commitments,* and *principles* are constantly used in the field of international relations for analytical descriptive, persuasive, and controversial purposes. Their shifting meanings are among the first difficulties that arise when the purpose is analytical. Then, as in the social sciences generally, the handicaps of an inexact terminology are quickly felt. The need for greater precision, however, has to be balanced against the equal need to communicate effectively on matters that concern not only specialists but everyone.

By way of caution, it should be stated that an overemphasis

[12] *Major Problems of United States Foreign Policy,* 1953–1954, the Brookings Institution, Washington, D.C., pp. 373–75.

on terminology can lead to the obscuring or oversimplification of the complex and dynamic nature of international relations. It is recognized that *interests* are frequently interlocked and that *objectives, policies,* and *commitments* are often difficult to disengage analytically without doing violence to reality. Because of their continuing nature, national interests can be and are popularly identified with objectives and policies of diverse kinds. Yet over a sufficiently long period of time, and in spite of choppings and changings, objectives and policies seem to fall into a comprehensible pattern that partially reveals the underlying national interests by which they have been given their particular forms. Though such a pattern must be accepted with reserve, it is nevertheless useful as a tentative hypothesis of what actually guides states along certain courses of action.

National interests may be defined as the general and continuing ends for which a nation acts. They embrace such matters as the need of a society for security against aggression, the desirability to a society of developing higher standards of living, and the maintenance of conditions of stability both nationally and internationally. The particular form of words in which national interests are stated is a product of changing social habits and values, and it reflects the experience as well as the expectations and aspirations of the nation's people. Despite changing modes of expression, national interests are the constants rather than the variables of international relations. They are durable and few in number, and they provide the broad frame of reference by which objectives are defined and policies developed.

National interests, as the essential framework for the definition of objectives and the conduct of policy, are conditioned by the geographical location of the state, shaped by the network of power relationships in which the state has developed, and expressed in terms that reflect the historical experience of the peoples concerned. Definitions of national interests tend to acquire the character and force of traditional habits of thought and understanding and they are not easily modified.

It should be observed that though the term *national interests* has sometimes been criticized on the ground that it implies self-seeking at the expense of others, no such connotation is intended here. National interests exist, and foreign policy would be conducted in a vacuum if it ignored them. Yet the existence of national interests does not preclude the acceptance of international obligations. Under present conditions, acceptance by a state of agreed international obligations may conceivably be the best guarantee of its national interests.

Objectives derive from national interests, but they are conditioned by the need to come to terms with the national interests of other states. In consequence of this interplay, objectives come to designate the particular kinds of adjustments sought, and hence the particular ends of policy.

When a national interest—either because it is felt to be threatened or because a pressure of expectation within a state brings it into sharp focus—becomes sufficiently compelling for a state to seek to establish it with finality by the active exercise of power or influence, it is delimited and particularized for a given context; it becomes an objective. If it were possible, at any given moment, to identify and correlate all the objectives of all the policies that a state is formulating and implementing, a picture would emerge of how a state believes that its national interests can best be guarded or forwarded under existing conditions.

Policies are specific courses of action designed to achieve objectives. For analytical purposes, policies can be regarded as means and objectives as ends. Since policies always develop in relation to actual situations and current problems, there is a greater degree of flexibility inherent in the formulation and application of policies than in the establishment of objectives. In popular usage, policy is often made synonymous with objectives and even with interests. It should be recognized that some policies have had so long a life that they have acquired a traditional standing. When this happens, a policy takes on some of the conceptual qualities of an objective or a national interest. In these circumstances, the modification of a policy is likely to be attended by a politically dangerous upsetting of established expectations. It should be added that policies vary greatly in scope and duration. Some, established over a long period of time, such as the Open Door policy in China, become deeply rooted; others come to an end as soon as the particular situation they are designed to meet undergoes significant change.

Commitments denote specific undertakings in support of a particular policy. Commitments may be vague or precise depending on circumstances, but in either event they represent fixed points in the application of policies. In popular language a commitment is often used loosely and interchangeably for a policy. The two terms are not interchangeable as used in this volume.

Principles, as a term used in the analysis of international relations, does not readily lend itself to precise definition. Nevertheless, the persistency with which the word has been and continues to be used in connection with the international conduct of states is not merely accidental. A strong sense of proper action, or a sense of dismay at action presumed to be wrong is so constantly revealed in the responses of peoples to the courses proposed or taken by governments that the existence and importance of standards of conduct and rules of action play a significant part in international relations. Although principles cannot be easily identified and are often demonstrably ignored, they represent the more or less clearly formulated patterns of behavior that guide national action and to which interests, objectives, and policies tend to conform. As sources of action, principles are deeply imbedded in the cultural patterns and political philosophy of a people. In spite of their sources being so intangible, principles sometimes achieve traditional formulations and then come to act almost as objectives and to give rise to specific policies.

To summarize: *interests* are what a nation feels to be essential to its security and well-being; *objectives* are interests spelled out and made more precise in the light of a current pattern of international relations; *policies* are thought out courses of action for achieving objectives; and *commitments* are specific undertakings in support of a given policy. Principles denote the judgments of value and guides to action by which a nation measures the suitability of its own objectives and policies and judges the objectives and policies of other states.

A final possible distinction should be kept in mind: the distinction between the foreign policy of a nation and a nation's foreign policies. The latter term is used only in the sense defined above for policies. The former is used to refer to the complex and dynamic political course that a nation follows in relation to other states. The foreign policy of a nation is more than the sum total of its foreign policies, for it also includes its commitments, the current forms of its interests and objectives, and the principles of right conduct that it professes.

PART 2

CHAPTER IV

Ideology and Objectives

Culture, Ideology and Foreign Policy

WE CONCLUDED our introductory part with a proposition that study of foreign policy consists of three mutually interdependent parts: ideology and objectives, factors, and policies. The study of factors and policies lends itself better to empirical method than do ideology and objectives. Facts in the latter area are more easily observable, more concrete, more descriptive. Study of ideologies and objectives in foreign policy borders on problems of non-empirical quality. Why is the study of ideologies relevant to understanding of foreign policies?

Foreign policy is not made by a "United States, Russia, France, India or Great Britain," by an abstract political deity. It is made by men. Foreign policy is a social process released by men, made by men, based on decisions arrived at by men. The decision in policy-making is an important station in this process. It is one of the precipitants, point of release of a significant political action. Men who make the decisions and execute the policies are motivated by certain interests and ideas. There is no foreign policy without an ideology; more, there are no men without ideologies.

Anthropologists will argue that culture is this element, which distinguishes men from animals. Animals have no culture. Ernst Cassirer sees the basic human element in symbolism. Symbolism is a part of culture as ideologies are. Certainly we do not know any animals which have or produce

57

ideologies as man does. We do not know any human group
without an idea system. The most primitive people, like the
Australian aborigines or the pygmies of Central Africa have
their religion, their magical practices, political concepts,
closely connected and interwoven. Biological needs are of
course fundamental in understanding human motivation. In
the same geographical environment, however, basic needs
are satisfied in different ways, and it may happen that the
Arapaho Indians, who live on the Wind River Reservation,
abundant in beautiful rainbow trout, do not catch fish. The
Hindu worships the cow while we drink cow's milk. Cultural
values rooted in idea-systems influence, often control satisfaction of our needs.

Primitive tribes had and have their foreign policies, of
course, too. Economic factors, such as hunting grounds, were
very important, and of fundamental significance in wars of
the Plains Indians. Religious beliefs, magic practices, however, influenced those relations, too. Status and role problems,
reflected in the unpleasant custom of scalp collecting, were
also a factor in foreign policies of the Plains Indians—not so
of those who sold the knives. Scalping also has an interesting
economic byline. George Catlin, who explored the Indian
country between 1832 and 1839, wrote: "the scalping knives
and tomahawks are of civilized manufacture, made expressly
for Indian use, carried into Indian country . . . and sold at
an enormous price . . . it is a common and cheap butcher
knife . . . manufactured in Sheffield in England, perhaps
for six pence; and sold to the poor Indian in this wild region
for a horse." An Indian had a different ideology from the
producer in Sheffield. In the hands of an Indian this butcher
knife was carving out strange objectives of his strange foreign
policy. A very important objective of Aztec foreign policy
was prisoners, taken for the purpose of religious sacrifice.
Their foreign policy decisions were determined by their religious ideology. Indeed, it is hard to analyze such policy
solely with the equipment of Hegelian and Marxian dialecti-
cal apparatus. Satisfaction of biological needs might have
affected relations with other primitive neighbors in Central

Africa, Australia or among the Plains Indians. The ways, however, in which it affected the process of decision-making, were influenced by their whole idea-system. Not everything can be explained by proteins.

After the Chinese Revolution, according to Pavlovsky, the Chinese government suggested that the Mongolian Khutuktu join the Chinese Republic. The Mongol Khutuktu answered that, in view of "Mongol customs and habits, which are different," it is better to live separately.[13] Whether sincerely or not, the Mongol ruler suggested that culture, ideology is different, and that it determines foreign policy. When the Russian-Mongol treaty had to be signed in November, 1912, the Russian delegates waited all day. Finally the Mongol representatives arrived, at 10 o'clock that night, and explained that the astrologer consulted had fixed this hour as the most happy one.[14] Choice of time was here decided within a cultural context, especially the idea-system of this culture, belief in astrology.

It is impossible to understand medieval foreign policy without knowledge, understanding, of thoughtways, idea-systems, beliefs, values of those who made foreign policy at that time. Politics of the papacy was and is above all a foreign policy. Men who made this policy had certain thoughtways; they had an idea-system, an ideology. They were making those decisions as a result of their religious-political ideology. It was theopolitics. Such an ideology corresponds in foreign policy to certain interests (not necessarily solely economic).

Interests are reflected in ideologies; and, in turn, values, ideologies influence interests and policy objectives. It is a functional, interactional relation. Values are reflected in policy objectives. India is overpopulated; so is Japan. In a certain historical period values, ideologies of Japanese ruling class were reflected in interpretation of interests, and, in consequence, in foreign policy objectives. The Japanese government has chosen a road of expansion. Overpopulation may

[13] Michel W. Pavlovsky, *Chinese Russian Relations*, Philosophical Library, New York, 1949, p. 49.
[14] op. cit. p. 50.

have contributed to it. Similarly, ideology, values of the Indian government are reflected in interpretation of their interests and in objectives. The ruling Congress Party of overpopulated India has not chosen a road of expansion to solve its problems. Ideology of a Ghandiist government is different from an ideology of a militaristic-nationalistic one. The difference is reflected in objectives, and in interpretation of interests.

Understanding and analysis of contemporary foreign policies requires knowledge, understanding of political ideologies. To understand nazi foreign policy, to analyze it properly, we had to know, along with other numerous factors, the nazi political ideology. The expansionist foreign policy is a part of nazi and fascist ideology, as global communist rule was a part of communist, Leninist ideology. War, as a means to achieve their expansionist goal, was glorified by nazis and fascists. Hitler's and Mussolini's foreign policy objectives were a part of nazi and fascist ideology. Means by which those ends had to be achieved were stated with candor. Similarly, in Lenin's and Stalin's writings, even in writings of "deviationists" such as Bukharin, Radek, the objectives of communist, Soviet foreign policy were stated. It was, and is impossible to discover the *long range*, or strategic nazi or communist foreign policy objectives without knowledge and understanding of their ideologies. One may argue that definite economic interests were behind the nazi foreign policy—that big business supported Hitler's politics, at least in the initial stage. All right then, those economic interests were reflected and may be discovered in the ideology, and in editorial policies of nazi papers.

American democracy is an ideology, and conduct of foreign affairs was also determined by this ideology. Wilson's concepts and vision of self-determination of nations is one of its elements. Economic interests of certain groups were of course reflected in United States foreign policy. So were they in the ideology and objectives of foreign policy, in ideology of statesmen, to mention here such ideological symbols as the "Big Stick" policy in Latin America or "Open Door" in

Asia. Change in ideology and objectives was also reflected in the conduct of foreign policy. "Big Stick" policy was displaced by "Good Neighbor" policy, and "Point 4," technical assistance for underdeveloped areas. One may argue that at the turn of the century American business guided the foreign policy of the American government, while thirty years later, under President Roosevelt and Truman, American government has guided and controlled "foreign policies" of American business.

Ideology: an Individual and Society

There is a continuous interaction between the individual and society, and in consequence between political ideas of an individual and political ideas of a society. It is impossible to separate the political ideas of an individual from those of society. Causal interpretation can hardly be used here. It is a dynamic, functional relationship, a continuous interaction. Similarly, the choice of political ideas of an individual is a result of his interaction between his personality structure and an interest in the society, social-economic environment, political conditions on the other hand and, culture. Every man, it was mentioned, has an ideology which he acquires from the society he is born into, through the process of socialization. We shall call the whole social ideology of a group "cultural idea-system." Political idea-systems are that part of a cultural-idea system, which is related to state, politics and society. There are many, not one, political idea-systems within the same cultural idea-system. A child acquires religious beliefs, later political concepts from his family, playmates, school. Ideas are not inborn; they are socially acquired. In more advanced societies, there is a variety, a differentiation of idea-systems, whether religious or political, while in primitive societies ideas are well integrated and uniform. In higher societies there is a possibility of choice of ideologies by an individual. Economic, political, social interest, personality structure, unique traumatic experience as a consequence of religious, national, racial discrimination, hunger, or similar events—all these may contribute to choice of a political creed.

Political ideology of an individual is often integrated with his whole outlook, the whole ideology (Germans call it Weltanschauung), his personality. Often men are inconsistent, and they believe simultaneously in ideologies which are contradictory. Ambivalence is not an exception—it is a frequent phenomenon. Fascists and nazis who preached persecution and war, professed also Christianity, similarly as some believe in race discrimination and in the American Bill of Rights.

The cultural idea-system, (as well as the culture of which the latter is a part) of an individual influences his political ideology. Concepts of history and time may influence political ideology and foreign policy objectives. Man in our culture is trying to assert himself. The heroic concept of life exercised its influence upon individuals throughout history. Alexander the Great, Napoleon, and many others were motivated by historical concepts, by desire to establish milestones in history, extend their memory—we call it glory—in time and space. They were mortals who desired eternity on earth, among men. Their concept of greatness, glory, their idea of relation of men to time, to history— their "historicism" influenced also their foreign policy objectives. Man struggled against his own oblivion by war and death—by oblivion of others. His struggle was mirrored in his ideas, and in foreign policies.

In Central Eastern European politics, the tragic past, translated into historicism, played a significant role, influencing political ideologies and affecting foreign policies. Here, the past in many respects determined the future. After 1918, Eastern European statesmen were trying to solve the problem from the vantage of the past. Joseph Pilsudski had a vision of Polish borders prior to 1772, prior to partitions. He and his followers were trying to recreate not an ethnographic but a historical Poland. Education and attitudes of his generation were deeply rooted in historical past, in the memories of the struggles and sufferings of the Poles. It was a generation of Poles which thought in historical terms, rather than in ethnographic, or even economic terms. The American statesman, the American thinker, the American student is interested in

new solutions, in the future, his emphasis is more on the
future than on the past. The League of Nations, the United
Nations, are visions which have stronger appeal to him than
has history. Foreign policy objectives are shaped within the
whole political idea-system, which in turn is a part of cultural
idea-system and of the whole culture. It is hardly possible to
understand foreign policy objectives without this cultural
perspective and, therefore, they should be analyzed within
the context to a society and culture.

Ideas and Politics

Ideas in politics have significance when shared by many,
by a group. The idea-systems have definite sociological functions, already discovered by the French sociologist Emile
Durkheim. Ideas are a cement which binds a society together.
Without ideas, society cannot exist. Without ideas, a political party cannot exist either. Goals are rooted in those
ideas; the whole sense of the group, interest—economic or
spiritual—is reflected in them. Ideas are a motivating force
in politics. In modern society political idea-systems, political
theories are developed by specialists, called "theoreticians"
in the continental European movement. Political ideology
becomes in that way an organized body of theory, continuously discussed, developed, advanced. Theory and ideology
contain goals of foreign and domestic policy. Democracy,
fascism, socialism, communism, zionism, anarchism—all those
"ideisms" have developed a considerable body of theory. In
our cultures, one culture, one culture idea-system usually
germinates not one, but many political idea-systems, some of
them controversial; some, in parts, in certain situations, overlapping.

Ideological Concepts

We have here used the term "ideology" in a broad sense,
and for our purpose we shall continue to define in that way
the wide area of the world of ideas. In a more detailed, specialized study, we may imagine more refined, precise terms.
The term "ideology," as we use it now, embraces a complex

and wide area. Within this area the term "ideology" could be reserved for a science of ideas—a study of origin of ideas, their analysis, problems of causation, similarly as the term "sociology" is used for science of society. Ideography (similar to ethnography, sociography) may correspond to a purely descriptive approach to problems of ideas. "Ideism," an awkward term (we could not find a better one), may serve to define beliefs in systems of ideas, definite political idea-systems such as "federalism," "nationalism," "socialism," "anarchism," "communism"—those "isms" and "ideisms." "Cultural idea system" is the whole "Weltanschauung" of an individual as member of a definite culture—whether Zuñi, Hopi, or French or German,[15] "political idea-system"—ideas related to the state.

A repetition of our analysis of a structure of political ideology, of an "ideography" might be useful for our purpose. Analysis of structure is relevant for a discussion of strategy and tactics.

In political "ideisms," in a political idea system, certain structural uniformities can be discovered. Those uniformities are significant, as they are helpful in analysis and in identification of foreign policies, especially in discovery of long-term goals.

Anatomy of a Political Ideology[16]

A political and social ideology as a basis of man's Weltanschauung, employing Webster's definition of that term—man's attitude to the surrounding world and explanation of the purpose of the world as a whole—is a typically European phenomenon.

A political ideology is a system of political, economic, and social values and ideas from which objectives are derived. These objectives form the nucleus of a political program.

Political ideologies, although more or less elaborate, are more or less consistent as well. Some are only outlined, such as peas-

---

[15] Our distinction of various ideological terms is a common result of an exchange of views with Professor Rex Hopper.

[16] Reprinted from "European Ideologies" (Chapter 1, Feliks Gross, Mechanics of European Politics), New York, 1949.

ant ideologies of eastern Europe (with the exception of Russia); others, such as Socialism, Communism, and Anarchism are thoroughly elaborated down to the most subtle details. Often they form a complete, harmonious, and consistent system of explanation of the purpose of society and of the surrounding social, economic and political phenomena. Setting forth dynamic and practical objectives to influence future social and political developments, they try—with a most ambitious design—to decide mankind's destiny.

A system of values and philosophy forms an underlying part of ideology, but economic, social, and political systems are an essential part, as well. Derived from the system of values, they are closely connected with the underlying philosophy. Such well-developed methods as Marxism aid in analyzing a current, concrete historical situation, and build a logical political program as a consequence of this broad analysis. A political program, then, is merely the outgrowth of a wide, detailed ideology, such as socialism or communism, or a less elaborate one, such as nationalist or peasant movements. The program is a formulation of immediate and practical political propositions for the attainment of concrete objectives: social, economic, or political which, in turn, are derived from the entire ideology.

We shall call ideology with a program, an ideological system. The reader may find it advisable to follow the analysis of the structure of European ideology by comparing this text with the chart of the structure shown on page 66.

An ideology contains many objectives which could be placed in a particular order to assume a hierarchy of importance. The final economic or political objectives may envisage a complete change in society: a change in economy from capitalist into collectivist, as in socialism, or a change from a state into a federation of communes, as in the anarchistic ideal. Practical objectives, or reform objectives (termed simply "reforms" in continental Europe), deal with immediate changes and improvements such as social security, eight-hour working days, protection of minorities, etc. Some movements lack any great final objectives or solutions, but their essence forms the practical goal or objective—the reform. Final objectives are a kind of social myth; reforms are closer to life.

Reforms often pave the way to the final objectives. The attainment of a higher standard of living, the limitation of working-hours—all these restrain economic exploitation more and more, and they form a portion of the final solution. The complete abolition of exploitation is the goal of social progress; it is the final objective of a democratic ideology.

The leading European ideologies have unfolded great visions—social myths—and attainable, final solutions in the form of integrated plans of social and political change.

Democracy, socialism, anarchism, communism, nationalism,

TABLE III

Structure of a European Ideological System

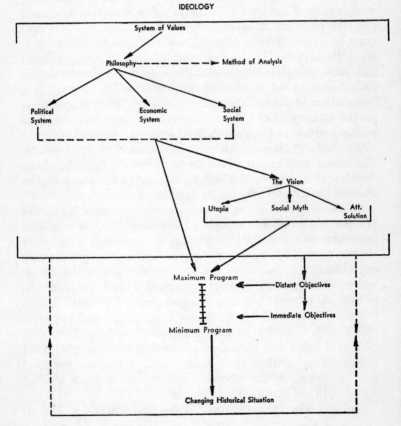

French Jacobinism, radical agrarian ideologies and Zionism—all these originated in Europe. Just as Buddhism, Christianity, Judaism, Islam, and all great world religions were born in Asia and the Eastern Mediterranean, so were all great political ideologies born in Europe out of that continent's misery, oppression, distress, wars, and revolutions.

From the viewpoint of a democratic and libertarian value system, the Utopian and visionary character of an ideology plays both a positive and a negative role, simultaneously.

The positive role of a social myth lies in its potentiality as an ideological stimulus. Utopianism contributed to the dynamic qualities of democracy and labor movements; visionary schemes and social myths have fostered political and social thought as well as practical social and economic planning. Cooperative, Socialist and similar visions contained moral values; they were capable of inspiring the masses to a higher objective, to the ideal of social justice and equality. Visionary schemes of an ideal, socialistic state and a society of justice and equality have found many ardent supporters willing to make high sacrifices for an ethical ideal.

But Utopianism and visionary schemes were equally important instruments in the development of totalitarian movements. A Utopian picture was painted for the masses, and they were asked to make sacrifices for it: sacrifices of freedom and of civil rights. They were brought to a peak of exaltation where they prepared temporarily to renounce their rights for the sake of a remote idea which could be attained, their persuaders assured them, within a short time if they were willing to pay the price—a temporary sacrifice of liberty. Hitler asked for greater power for himself and his gang. He dangled the prize of a Utopia, a perfect German state. Each German resident would be a member of a privileged race (Herrenrasse) riding in a Volksauto! Hitler demanded that Germany's entire energy should be concentrated upon the attainment of this goal. In the Soviet Union, a temporary dictatorship of the proletariat—in fact, of the individual—was considered merely a transitory step towards a Soviet Utopia. "Wait five years—we shall accomplish that!"

Utopias, visions, and social myths formed an important stimulus for democratic movements, but they were equally successful in enlisting the support of the masses for totalitarian leaders.

However, the distant vision, the final solution or social myth must not necessarily always be a Utopia; a number of solutions which appeared to be Utopias were operated with varying degrees of success as practical propositions. A free association of nations was an age-old Utopia, and an unattainable dream, but the League of Nations and the United Nations organization became a reality. Today, world government is still a perfectionist dream, but its reality some time in the future can be safely predicted. A state without private industry was once regarded as a social myth, but this Utopia has been put into operation, as have states with combined socialized and private industries.

The social myth envisions the perfect society, a plan which may be removed from immediate reality and appears unattainable to the present generation; often, it is an attractive picture of a distant future.

There is little difference between Utopia and social myth; a difference rather in quantity than quality. Utopia contains more phantasy; it seems to be still more unreal and visionary than social myth.

Let us call a practical, final solution an attainable plan such as the transformation of a landowner's feudal state into a cooperative peasant state through radical land reform: this was a practical plan for Hungary. Or, let us use this term for the conversion of a Kingdom into a democratic Republic: this was an attainable plan for Greece. Thus, we can divide all political visions into Utopias, social myths, and practical, final solutions. However, it is extremely difficult to draw a sharp line between Utopias and practical, final solutions. A Utopia, put into operation, may prove to be thoroughly practical and attainable, while a final solution, on the other hand, may prove impractical and Utopian!

An architect before drawing up definite plans for, let us say, a Rockefeller Center, envisions this beautiful monument of twentieth century architecture. Then, after having conceived a general picture in his mind, he makes blueprints which are later translated into the reality of stone and concrete and organized into a harmonious entity.

Similarly, an economic or political planner first conceives a visionary plan such as, for instance, the first Five Year Plan. From it he prepares a practical blueprint with figures, statistics, and concrete proposals. Such a blueprint is later placed into operation. Even the cautious planner cannot definitely ascertain the outcome. Just as the paper-beautiful plans of an architect may produce, against his volition, an ugly edifice which will be outmoded within a few years, so a social and economic plan which appears logical, consistent, and harmonious may display glaring defects when translated into reality. Thus, a visionary, perfect plan—a practical, final solution may show serious deficiencies and emerge a failure instead of a success. More practical, less impressive, and less inspired plans sometimes prove more workable when attempted. In brief, practicability is the only true test of a beautiful vision.

Partisans of such well-developed ideologies as socialism or communism have developed essential and subtle distinctions between broad ideologies and programs. In European politics particularly, since they have been deeply influenced by great, well-developed ideologies for more than a century, this distinction is of real significance.

Ideologies of Foreign and Domestic Policies

Political parties do not have a schizophrenic idea-system— one for foreign, another for domestic policy. Both, as we see later, are closely interconnected and mutually inter-dependent; they form an entity. In the nazi political idea-system the Utopia—the vision of the Third Reich—was a vision of both a domestic and a foreign policy. This meant German domination over Europe. Germany conceived as the political and industrial center of the world. In the Communistic idea-system, foreign policy objectives—world Communist system— are part of the total, political ideology. Representatives of totalitarian governments, propagandists of those systems, usually kept assuring us that their domestic policy has nothing to do with foreign policies, that foreign policies would remain unchanged. There were always naive ones to believe. However, the words of propagandists and diplomats of Hitler, Mussolini, and Stalin were solely tools, tools used to deceive public opinion, to disarm neighbors morally and materially, to prepare, behind this smokescreen of words, the conquest, invasion, and domination of the weaker.

Indeed, it was not too hard for Hitler to convince Neville

Henderson or Neville Chamberlain about "peace in our time"; neither was it difficult to convince Colonel Beck about Hitler's peaceful intentions. First of all, they wanted to be convinced. They themselves looked for psychological escape into false security.

Those "convincing" arguments on different objectives of domestic and foreign policies run through well-established traditional channels. For centuries jurists carefully divided domestic from foreign affairs. Foreign relations were regarded by them as entirely separate, different activities. States, in diplomatic semantics, became objects, subjects, persons. International relations became in such an approach relations, not between societies, but between some kinds of individuals. Domestic politics, as a consequence of the concept of national sovereignty, were not touched by correct negotiations, diplomats, and students of foreign politics. However ideologies on domestic affairs affected as a rule foreign policy objectives. Religious wars are a good evidence. Religious struggle within a country had effect on its foreign policy objectives. Hence religious war as a result of those idea-conflicts, and famous accommodation—*cuius regio–eius religio*—affected foreign policies, international relations. In foreign policy analysis an understanding of the *whole* political ideology is relevant. Only through such approach may we discover final, strategic objectives of a party, ruling group, or political movement in power.

The very discussion of foreign policy, even clarification of the objectives, usually produces immediate effects inside and outside of a state. In a democracy discussion of a foreign policy is no secret. Parliamentary debates are open to the public and the policy statements are continuously released by secretaries of state and foreign ministers. The whole process which leads to new foreign policies affects the public opinion as well as the policies of all the countries concerned. The famous Point Four policy had such an effect when it was stated, that even communist controlled governments of captive countries fell under its spell. Fears were expressed that the "new look" policy of the United States, based on retaliation, would have disturbing psychological effects as much among our friends as our opponents.

The Vision

Social myths, utopias are elements of ideology also in the area of international relations. Long-range foreign policy objectives are usually part of a vision. We use the terms ideology and utopia here in a different way from Karl Mannheim. Mannheim uses the term "ideology" for the present, existing idea-system, "utopia" for the future objectives, future social image. We use here the term "vision" for Mannheim's concept of utopia. We used the terms utopia, social myths, practical solutions, in reference to practicability, to an extent conformity of vision or its "phantasy." But there is still another element which has to be considered. Social myths and utopias are—from the point of view of present experience, conformity—more distant from present reality than attainable, practical solution. They have the element of the fabulous, of phantasy, of imagination, often beauty of distant, non-real worlds. They also have an appeal to the emotions and potentiality to capture the imagination of masses. Georges Sorel was one of the first to realize the significance of social myths[17] as a motor of mass movements. Social myth, utopia unfolds distant, mysterious social images. Practical solutions are pragmatic. Some are more "visionary," others with their "feet on the ground," real and rational like even and odd pages of a bank account. If they are too pragmatic, they may lose their appeal. Bank books may have appeal to an individual—they do not appeal to mass movements.

Some of the utopias or social myths, once abstract, visionary, distant, become realities; they turn out to work, to be attainable. The idea of self-determination of nations, Mazzini's ideals, those of Polish, Hungarian, or Czech patriots, were distant, unreal dreams, vision. Tsar Alexander I said to the Poles "no dreams." Indeed independent Poland, in the first decade of the XIX century was a dream, as independent

[17] Georges Sorel, introduction to *Réflexions sur la Violence*, Paris, 1946 edition.

Bohemia was a utopia in times of Metternich. The great Wilsonian vision however, self-determination of nations—national states associated in a League of Nations—became a fact.

The beauty of the ideal and myth is often destroyed by crude realities, so different from our phantasy. Such was the case of 1918's self-determination of nations, of difficulties of those nations, weakness and cruel conquest by ruthless neighbors. The reality was different from social myth. But the vision had a powerful motivating force. In Russian foreign policy the vision called "Third Rome" provided a psychological and political appeal to certain social strata.

"Third Rome" and the flow of pilgrims to the Holy Land are an example of visions, even religion as a motivating force of certain groups of populations, of social forces—directed toward political objectives in foreign policy. The vision, of course, contained the very objectives—expansion of the Russian state toward Constantinople and the middle East. The social myth of Third Rome was already here at the end of the fifteenth century—and was expressed in a letter of Philoteus, Abbot of Pskov to Ivan III, ". . . as to the second Rome —the church of Constantinople—it has been hewn by the axes of Ishmaelites, but this third new Rome—the Holy Apostolic church under thy mighty rule shines throughout the entire world . . ."[18]

In 1915, during secret negotiations in London, Russian foreign minister Serge Sazanov expressed interest in Palestine. "For centuries," he wrote, in his memoirs, "an endless stream of pilgrims from Russia went to the Holy Land, Russian pilgrims outnumbered those from all other Christian countries taken together. Consequently, the Orthodox Palestine Society was formed . . . spread a network of religious and educational institutions throughout Palestine and part of Syria. . . ."

" . . . According to the general rule that in the East everything is in one way or another connected with politics, these

[18] Paul Miliukov, "Outlines of Russian Culture", Ed. by Michael Karpovich, translated by V. Ughet and E. Davis, University of Pennsylvania Press, 1948, p. 15.

institutions, essentially non-political, acquired a certain political significance as indicative of Russian influence. . . ."[19]

Practical, pragmatic solutions are visions too. Such is a
British pragmatic vision of balance of power in Europe, or
Washington's, Jefferson's, Monroe's more imaginative vision
of a United States free of European intrusions, protected by
oceans, peaceful and avoiding any European entanglements.

Vision, as a concept of a social image, as a motivating
force, as "locus" of foreign policy objectives, may never be
attained but it is a guiding star, like the North Star for the
sailor. Those visions provide directions of foreign policies, or
provide tools to motivate masses in support of those visions,
support in war, conquest, or peace and cooperation. Sometimes, a cynical government may not believe in a social myth
which it manipulates. It might be cynical, and harbour goals
of its own for which a utopia was painted. A utopia, a social
myth, however, motivates the people which they govern,
moves the people to action, makes them willing to die. To
provide this strong emotional intoxicant, a vision has to have
the irrational, the distant, the heroic, unreal. It has to be a
"utopia," a "social myth."

Visions contain long-range objectives. In American tradition, a vision is usually formulated within a concrete situation; we may call such formulation a "doctrine." Such a doctrine usually carries a symbol; in other words, it is identified
by a symbol which has a broader appeal—to mention the
Monroe Doctrine, Open Door, 14 Points, Good Neighbor,
Atlantic Charter, Truman Doctrine. All those symbols identify doctrines.

The Irrational

There is, however, an element in a social myth which is
absent in pragmatic, practical proposition. It is the specific
appeal of social myth to the broad masses, even to the same
ruling group, which may manipulate the social myth. Social
myth has an irrational element, has a psychological sparkle,

[19] Serge Sazanov, *"Fateful Years, 1909–1916,"* Stokes, New York, 1928,
pp. 256–258.

which concrete, massive, practical plans, with all empiricism and rationalism, lack. Social myth unfolds a vision, which to the sober seems unreal. But a seemingly unreal vision attracts those who are tired of long misery and persecution, who look for a fundamental change of their status of an oppressed nation. Here was the great appeal of nationalism, national liberation, a social myth of all nations free, democratic, respecting mutual rights. Such was the vision of the French Revolution in foreign politics. Indeed, the slogan embroidered on flags—*tutti uomini liberi sono fratelli*—had an appeal. Of similar quality was the vision of Mazzini and Wilson. The seemingly unreal social myth of eternal glory appeals to a believer, to whom politics becomes religion; such was the myth of Third Rome, for Russia. A social myth of happiness and wealth of Eldorado moved Spanish ships and motivated and guided Spanish sailors, armies and foreign politics to the perils and adventure of the great South American drama. A social myth of the once powerful, happy land of Israel was a vision of Zionism. It seems that this land was never very prosperous and fertile, but a memory of those better times was carefully preserved. Through 2000 years a vision, social myth of Zion, was alive. An Israel—a state of Jews—was it not a social myth, an unreal distant image, for those Jews beaten, humiliated in pogroms of Jassy or dying in camps of Dachau and Majdanek? Such a myth generated hopes, will for struggle, resistance, sacrifice! Once a myth became real, true, the charm was gone; at least a part of it. New visions, however, grew and generated their magic.

In certain culture social myths have greater appeal than in another. Why? It is hard to answer. The British have their vision—the empire—but on the whole they are much more restrained in accepting broad, unreal-looking visions. They are willing to try out a proposition and, if it works, all right—it is accepted. A proposition has to be, however, pragmatic, real, businesslike, not improvised, not an outburst of emotional enthusiasm. The British political psychology is reflected, for instance, in the attitude of major parties toward European Federation. Churchill in his Zurich speech in 1946 threw a great vision to Europe: the myth of a United States of Europe. Churchill's speech had more appeal among the French, Poles, Germans, Belgians than among the British. On the continent of Europe social myth has wider appeal. It is a continent which generates ideologies, social visions, schemes for perfect political systems. A practical statesman who tries to attain a practical goal, may as well translate his solution into a social myth, when he tries to appeal to those nations which are moved by a social myth more than by dry political outlines.

Social myth has its significance in foreign politics. It is an ignition which releases social forces. Of course those forces are already conditioned toward action by other social, economic, political factors. The vision, the ideological element may form a social-psychological precipitant. Since the religious wars, social forces—social-religious movements, or social-political movements—formed a powerful factor of foreign politics. The Nazis were able to attract large groups of German minorities in Poland, Czechoslovakia and other countries. They became an important factor in Nazi expansionist schemes. The Communist parties all over the world are an important factor of Soviet foreign policy. The social myth of an equalitarian state has its influence on parts of public opinion. Social myth in this case becomes a successful smoke-screen for a gigantic slave system of the Soviet Union with ten to fifteen million (if not more) in forced labor camps.

National Interest

The concept of "national interest" is an important part of foreign policy. It is located within the vision, within the social image of a desired international order. The concept of "national interest" is man-made; it is formulated by some leaders, theoreticians, accepted by a following, by a larger group. It is a social phenomenon—it reflects values, ideas, interests of a social group, as well as of its authors. They appear on electoral platforms in times of elections, rather as core of symbols, slogans, than elaborated theories. They are unfolded before the people as part of visions, "doctrines" such as the Truman Doctrine, Wilson's 14 Points.

Historians, political scientists, theoreticians with more or less clarity debate what a national interest is or should be. Often the views are opposed. The concept—a result of interest and ideologies—might be different in various ideologies and for various interests. The concept of national interest of de Gaulle and Laval in 1941–45 was different, although both were Frenchmen. The "bipartisan" concept of American foreign policy as well as, for a much longer period, the conduct of British foreign policy are both results of a happy compromise of opposing parties. Though opposed in domestic politics, the leadership of those parties searched for an agreement on principles and objectives of foreign policy; they searched and found a common denominator for the concept of "national interest" oriented rather to broad interests of its citizens, its people, than to limited narrow interests of definite groups. In European history, both concepts—"national interest" and "raison d'état," were often vague, intermixed with social myths—such as "mission of a nation" presented as dogmas, absolutes not subject to discussion called "imponderabilia." All those high-sounding words usually harbored interests and privileges of a dynasty, of an economic or political system, of a ruling group. This is especially true of dynastic systems, rooted in feudal survivals, of states ruled by extreme nationalists, advocating expansion.

The concept of "raison d'état," as the famous study of Meinecke indicates, is on the whole difficult to define.

In a democracy foreign policy should be guided by "raison de citoyens," reason of citizen, interest of citizen, rather than "raison d'état," reason of state, national interest.

Both concepts—national interest and reason of state—are of social, or cultural origin. They reflect the culture, idea-system, interest of social groups. With the change of society, change of culture, new concepts, may emerge. It seems to me that one of the underlying values of this idea will continue. This value is survival. Whatever the concept of national interest is, however misty and foggy the concept of reason of state, it means always survival of a state, of a nation, of a system, of a ruling group, of certain values—always survival either of ideas or of certain groups and their interests.

Interests and meaning of those ideas become more lucid, once they are discussed in a concrete, real context situation.

In certain cases the concept of national interests becomes more pragmatic, hard, real in terms of facts and numbers. When this happens, an impression is created that the concept of national interest is rational, empirical, free of any value judgment, subject to quantitative estimates in numbers, numbers of human life or even cynically in terms of dollars and cents.

Jefferson's concept of American national interest was, according to Charles A. Beard, the acquisition of adjacent areas as territories for further cultivation by American farmers.[20] Agriculture, according to Jefferson, was the way of life for a healthy and free republic. Charles A. Beard does not overlook the moral (we should say—ideological) aspects of the concept (p. 358) his emphasis is, however, on the political, economic aspects. But even this economic, political concept of Jefferson, of national interest, interest of the people is an ideological concept. Jefferson regarded agriculture as a basis of a democratic republic and this is ideology, a vision of a society. He gave preference to agriculture as such economics, according to Jefferson, contributed to stability and freedom. Hamilton's concept of national interest, as Beard indicates, was different and, of course, connected with different interests. During our midcentury, nations have been threatened with biological extermination. Biological survival becomes then a national interest which seems to be pragmatic, real, free of values. Here the interest was dictated by common sense—to save the "naked life." It seems no alternative for another formulation could be supplied. Struggle for foreign markets, raw materials is an empirical phenomenon, expressed in hard currency, material values. Still, those cases are not free from ideological influences and values. Imperial-

---

[20] Charles A. Beard, *The Idea of National Interest*, an Analytical Study in American Foreign Policy, Macmillan, New York, 1934, p. 550.

ism, expansion have their ideological content and values; not every "imperialism" can be identified with another one. British imperialism of the XIX century has a different ideological content, different values from the contemporary Soviet concept. The Poles were threatened with biological extinction by the Germans during World War II. Even in a situation of jeopardy, they had a choice: submission or resistance (we shall return to this problem in our discussion of population factors). Culture of a nation is reflected in its concept of national interest.

Whose National Interest?

The national interest of the Soviet rulers today might be entirely different from the interests of their subject peoples. The interest of a despotic government in its survival might be different from the interest as felt, though not expressed, by various groups, by the people. A despotic government may use the term "national interest"—and the term might be accepted at face value.

The discrepancy between an idea system, theories advocated by the leadership of a party, and ideas people really believe is a hardly explored issue. There might be a difference between what the government or leaders believe is a national interest and the opinion of the people, of the public opinion on the very same issue. As Lindsay Rogers in his penetrating book "The Pollsters" (Knopf, New York, 1949) indicated, there might be no opinion. The government might have an opinion as to what a national interest is, what the exigencies of the moment are, while the citizen may have no opinion, or may not even know what the situation is. Charles Beard calls national interest "the pivot of diplomacy." He quotes Alfred Thayer Mahan, that governments act continuously on no other ground than on the ground of national interest. Mahan further continues that governments must put as their objective the interests of their "own wards, their own people." What is the interest of the people? Who decides about it? The answer to this question, relevant in democracy, is continuously discussed rather by the leadership, theoreticians, experts than by the voters. Ideas are approved rather a posteriori, in an indirect way, through elections. Elections indicate consent rather on general principle, values, than on a detailed, elaborated concept of national interests.

Objectives and Doctrines

Objectives—strategic objectives or ends—form the kernel of our ideology. They are a result of the whole ideology and are formulated in such manner that they can be translated into actions (policies). Tactical objectives are designed with strategic objectives in mind. Their purpose is to achieve the latter. Our short-range objectives, are tactical objectives; they are also means; our long-range objectives are strategic objectives, or ends.

In American history, principles of conduct, values, national interest, objectives were clearly stated in form of "doctrines." When critical, historical situations called for candor in foreign policy, this was done in the form of declarations such as Monroe's Doctrine of 1823, Wilson's 14 Points, Open Door Doctrine, Good Neighbor Policy, Roosevelt's Four Freedoms, Truman's Containment Policy. Formulation of foreign policy as a definite doctrine is an old, established American tradition, since Washington's Farewell Address. A doctrine is a statement on objectives, national interest, principles, values in a concrete, definite situation. It is a cut through ideology—vision, national interest, objectives—within a context situation.

In the Monroe Doctrine of 1823, a *concrete situation* is indicated:

> . . . to arrange by amicable negotiation the respective rights and interests of the two nations on the northwest coast of this continent . . . The late events in Spain and Portugal show that Europe is still unsettled.

Values, principles, objectives are stated:

> . . . that the American continents, by the free and independent condition which they have assumed and maintain, are hence-

forth not to be considered as subject for future colonization by any European powers (*objectives*—negatively stated, *values*).

In the wars of the European powers in matters relating to themselves we have never taken any part, nor does it comport with our policy to do so. It is only when our rights are invaded or seriously menaced that we resent injuries or make preparation for our defense (*principles*).

. . . We owe it, therefore, to candor and to the amicable relations existing between the United States and those powers to declare, that we should consider any attempt on their part to extend their system to any portion of this hemisphere as dangerous to our peace and safety (*national interest*).

. . . Our policy in regard to Europe, which was adopted at an early stage of the wars which have so long agitated that quarter of the globe nevertheless remains the same, which is not to interfere in the internal concerns of any of its powers; to consider the government de facto as the legitimate government for us; to cultivate friendly relations with it . . . meeting in all instances the just claims of every power, submitting to injuries from none . . . (*principles*).

The reader will discover similar elements in carefully reading the "14 Points" of President Wilson, Roosevelt's "Four Freedoms" or Truman's "Doctrine" with the strategic objective of containment of further Communist advance.

Doctrines in American foreign policy are usually turning points in the conduct of foreign affairs. Who coins a symbol for a doctrine (Big Stick, Open Door) or selects them from a declaration? Who names it a "doctrine?" We have to leave this question to the future research in sociology and ethnography of foreign politics.

Objectives and principles are more often stated and restated in public declarations. They reinforce the position of government and in a democratic process serve an important purpose; namely, to inform and win public opinion. Restatement of objectives and principles is of major significance when declared by the Chief Executive. Such declarations are also made by secretaries of state, leaders of the opposing parties. The latter is of relevance, as it indicates discrepancy or unity in policies, objectives, principles.

In his address to the American Society of Newspaper Editors in Washington on April 16, 1953, President Eisenhower stated the principles of conduct of foreign policy:

The way chosen by the United States was plainly marked by a few clear precepts which govern its conduct in world affairs.

FIRST: No people on earth can be held—as a people—to be an enemy, for all humanity shares the common hunger for peace and fellowship and justice.

SECOND: No nation's security and well being can be lastingly achieved in isolation, but only in effective cooperation with fellow-nations.

THIRD: Any nation's right to a form of government and an economic system of its own choosing is inalienable.

FOURTH: Any nation's attempt to dictate to other nations their form of government is indefensible.

AND FIFTH: A nation's hope of lasting peace cannot be firmly based upon any race in armaments, but rather upon just relations and honest understanding with all other nations.

Afterwards, in the same address, he stated his objectives:

The first great step along this way must be the conclusion of an honorable armistice in Korea.

This means the immediate cessation of hostilities and the prompt initiation of political discussions leading to the holding of free elections in a united Korea.

It should mean—no less importantly—an end to the direct and indirect attacks upon the security of Indo-China and Malaya. For any armistice in Korea that merely released aggressive armies to attack elsewhere would be a fraud.

We seek, throughout Asia as throughout the world, a peace that is true and total.

Out of this can grow a still wider task—the achieving of just political settlements for the other serious and specific issues between the free world and the Soviet Union.

None of these issues, great or small, is insoluble—given only the will to respect the rights of all nations.

Again we say: The United States is ready to assume its just part.

We have already done all within our power to speed conclusion of a treaty with Austria which will free that country from economic exploitation and from occupation by foreign troops.

We are ready not only to press forward with the present plans for closer unity of the nations of Western Europe but also, upon that foundation, to strive to foster a broader European community, conducive to the free movement of persons, of trade and of ideas.

This community would include a free and united Germany, with a government based upon free and secret ballot.

This free community and the full independence of the East European nations could mean the end of the present unnatural division of Europe.

As progress in all these areas strengthens world trust, we could proceed concurrently with the next great work—the reduction of the burden of armaments now weighing upon the world. To this end we would welcome and enter into the most solemn agreements. These could properly include:

1. The limitation, by absolute numbers or by an agreed international ratio, of the sizes of the military and security forces of all nations.

2. A Commitment by all nations to set an agreed limit upon that proportion of total production of certain strategic materials to be devoted to military purposes.

3. International control of atomic energy to promote its use for peaceful purposes only, and to insure the prohibition of atomic weapons.

4. A limitation or prohibition of other categories of weapons of great destructiveness.

5. The enforcement of all these agreed limitations and prohibitions by adequate safeguards, including a practical system of inspection under the United Nations.

The details of such disarmament programs are manifestly critical and complex. Neither the United States nor any other nation can properly claim to possess a perfect, immutable formula. But the formula matters less than the faith—the good faith without which no formula can work justly and effectively.

Former President Truman in his speech on the Four Freedoms stated the objectives on September 29, 1953.

We have to understand the basic pillars of our American foreign policy, and support them, regardless of partisanship. We have to know them when we see them. And I suggest that they are as follows:

A renewed and reinvigorated reciprocal trade program.

A strong defense—a really strong defense, one that means something.

Support of the North Atlantic Treaty.

Support of European unity.

Support of the Rio Pact.

Support of the Pacific alliances.

Technical assistance and economic aid for the underdeveloped countries.

The willingness, in firm agreement with our allies and from a position of united strength, to seek in all sincerity solutions of our differences with the Soviet bloc through patient and peaceful negotiations.

And finally, my friends, the whole-hearted support of the United Nations.

Objectives and principles in both statements are similar. Ribbentrop in a letter to Stalin (Berlin, October 13, 1940) presents the following vision and objectives:[21]

In summing up, I should like to state that, in the opinion of the Führer, also, it appears to be the historical mission of the Four Powers—the Soviet Union, Italy, Japan, and Germany—to adopt a long-range policy and to direct the future development of their peoples into the right channels by delimitation of their interests on a world-wide scale.

The concept of "historical mission" is a social myth. What is the meaning of a "mission?" Who gave Hitler a mandate for this mission? Providence? Ribbentrop uses here, however, the basic tools—concepts of objectives, vision, policies.

A government may face a situation in which a choice between objectives has to be made. We may have more objectives than one: a hierarchy of objectives. A choice of objectives by the policy makers is determined according to their significance. Less important ones have to be postponed, or abandoned in favor of those of higher urgency.

A political agreement on principles and objectives in a

[21] *Nazi-Soviet Relations 1939–1941*, Department of State, 1948, p. 213.

current conduct of foreign policy is not necessarily identical, however, with general and permanent acceptance of definitions of what national interest and objectives are.

Dynamic Character of Basic Concepts

Our basic concepts such as national interest and objectives are dynamic. They are subject to discussions and to continuous reinterpretation and re-evaluation. Social-economic conditions are continuously changing. The rate of our present technological and social change is hardly comparable with any other period of our history; a similarity can be found solely in the revolutionary character of the industrial revolution. All this has its effects on concepts of foreign policy. A recent meeting of the American Academy of Political and Social Science (April 18–19, 1952) devoted to the problem of national interest indicated wide difference in views and expressed also trends toward re-interpretation of the concept of national interest in American foreign policy. The general topic of the meeting "The National Interest—Alone or with Others?" was an admission of discrepancy of views and acknowledgment of significance of basic concepts. A sharp difference exists between the "realists" and the "idealists." The approach of the latter is also called a "legalistic-moralistic" approach. The vision of the realists is balance of power, while the idealists' vision is a new world order, based on international organization and law.

George Kennan and Hans Morgenthau represent the realistic school. Morgenthau formulates the interest of the United States in "terms of national security and integrity of American experiment." The objective of national interest conceived that way is position and security of the United States in the Western Hemisphere, which can be maintained by European and Asiatic balance of power. The essence of foreign policy, argues Morgenthau, remains the same; circumstances have changed.

The idealists derive their ideology from the great Wilsonian traditions. Their basic objective is rule of law and moral principles in international relations. The national interest of the United States, United States security can be preserved at best in an international world order guided by law and moral principles. These views were represented by Senator John Sparkman, the late A. Feller, by Norman Thomas, and C. B. Marshall. Marshall argues that: "we can serve our national interest only by a policy which transcends our national policy." Thomas: ". . . in today's world it is not merely a matter of ethics but of common sense to affirm that the true national interest can be served only with others. There is no nation . . . that is sufficient in natural resources. . . ."[22] Once security of the people of the United States requires co-operation and mutual support of other peoples, the national interest of the United States must take into account the interest of other nations. The French or British government may be willing to support a common interest of United States, France, or Great Britain. The French government may be willing to support American interests, as United States governments have consistently and generously supported the interests of the French people. However, by narrowing the concept of national interest to its own nation a government may lose friends and allies in strategic areas. A common denominator must be found—a common interest superior to a single one. Such were principally the concepts of Wilson, Roosevelt, Truman, Eisenhower; such were the great, historical lines of American foreign policy since 1918. In times of global foreign policy, in times of *world* politics the concept of national interest has been broadened, the leaders had to consider mutual relationship of national interests and the interest of world community, reconcile both in broadening the frames of narrowly conceived objectives and interests. It is beyond the scope of this book to argue one way or the other. What is significant, as far as our topic is concerned, is the fact of re-interpretation, re-evaluation of national interest. A re-interpretation of such a concept, adopted by a government

[22] "The National Interest—Alone or with Others?", edited by Norman D. Palmer, *Annals of the American Academy of Political and Social Science,* vol. 282, July 1952. See especially the introduction by Palmer, articles by: H. J. Morgenthau, J. Sparkman, N. Thomas, A. H. Feller, C. B. Marshall.

in power means a change in ideology—in consequence, a change on a strategic level. Such a change is relevant in any foreign policy analysis, so that even trends toward such a change have to be carefully studied, observed.

In recent discussion also the problem of power as an objective was a key issue of foreign policy analysis. Again, the realists took the lead in emphasizing significance of power as an objective. Morgenthau's contention is that power is always the immediate objective, even though the ultimate aim may be freedom, peace, security, prosperity.[23] Morgenthau's position could be easily misinterpreted. The core of his idea is that whatever goals we seek—moral or immoral—in international politics, power is essential, since without power, aims cannot be achieved. He advocates realism in politics, as objectives cannot be achieved without action, and without adequate power.[24]

Of course, power plays an important role in politics, and most political actions require power. An analyst, however, could hardly suggest the equation: power equals power. Power is expressed in economic, military, geographical and other potentialities. It is potential power. We may call "kinetic power" power in action. How the power will be used, in what direction released, if released at all, depends upon our ideology, values. The power of Stalin or Hitler does not equate with power of Aristides Briand. What is important is the purpose for which it is used, the goals, the objectives, ideology. Distinction between potentialities and use of power is relevant. Power of the United States government has not been used to conquer the Western Hemisphere, although in terms of power this was possible. Soviet advance, expansion has been stopped solely by consideration of power—while in ideologies of the American governments, especially since Wilson, use of power is restrained by law and moral consider-

[23] Hans J. Morgenthau, *Politics Among Nations,* Alfred A. Knopf, New York, 1948, p. 13. See also "In Defense of National Interest," Alfred A. Knopf, New York, 1951.
[24] See also Hans Morgenthau, "Another Great Debate: The National Interest of the United States," *Am. Pol. Science Review,* XLVI, Dec. 1952.

ation (Jefferson, Wilson). Power is used with restraint. It is not always used. Not once, but many times in recent American history the United States government did not use its power, potential power to enforce certain interests, in Central America, though this was done before by other United States governments. Physical power is not always a goal and it is not always, in all situations, exercised by a government. Some governments use more power, others less—though they may have the same potentialities.

Neither culture, nor of course a cultural ideology, nor political ideology are static, they change continuously, as society is changing, and society and culture cannot be separated. Political idea-systems and concepts of national interest change. They change when interest—social, economic, political, or cultural—changes. They change when economic situation changes—for instance, when a depression comes. They changed even more in times of the industrial revolution and subsequent struggle for markets. Change in economic and in social conditions affected political idea system and concepts of national interests. On the other hand, great ideological, religious changes such as Islam affected foreign policy outlook, contributing to an expansionist movement of Arab states. Change of interests affects the culture, political idea-systems and eventually also the strategic goals.

In every society are many political ideologies, many political parties, as there are various interests as well as there are non-shared values. Values shared by a whole nation form the basis of national culture, and cultural ideologies. Various interests which are different are reflected in different political movements, different political ideologies and different concepts of foreign policy.

Philosophy of International Relations

A vital area in study of foreign policy formulation is the problem of objectives, vision, of ideology—not solely what they are today, but what the desirable objectives, ideologies, are. In other words, what kind of a world we wish to see, what kind of international world order we would like to organize "what ought to be" as a next question, once we explored "what is." This area of discussion however is not any more a purely scientific one, in an empirical sense. The questions which have to be answered are connected with "right" and "wrong," "good" and "bad"—with norms, values. Such dilemmas have grown out of experience—experience which is empirical. The answer, however, puts a demand on our moral, ethical qualities, the answer belongs in large part to a field of political philosophy. A deeper study of idea-systems also involves non-empirical consideration, values. Study of idea-systems, at least certain aspects of it, belong to an area which was termed by Mannheim "relationist." As an observer, the analyst is not in a position to divorce himself from his values. Criticism of values, of ethical elements of an idea-system, is "relationistic."

According to most academicians, this area does not belong to the universities, as it involves ideological beliefs, political tendencies, even indoctrination. The traditional area of universities is the area of scientific exploration, exploration of facts, exploration of what is—not what ought to be. We cannot, however, escape the questions "what is possible," "what, under the circumstances, should be done," "what kind of international relations is desirable, granting that values and principles are a premise of such discussion." Not only choice of values and principles is normative but, in consequence, so is the choice of solutions, choice of our objectives in foreign politics. We are a part of society; the process of choice reflects our culture—true. It can be empirically described. But the decision, selection, choice of one of the solutions, out of many possibilities is again of normative character. No decision in foreign policy is possible without a value judgment ("right" solution) which is normative.

"Philosophy of international relations," may be an appropriate term for this area of ideology, visions, values, principles, future plans and solutions in the area of foreign politics. The philosophy of international relations is only a part of a wide field—social-political philosophy. The efforts of the well known Chicago group, the "Committee to Frame a World

Constitution," headed by Chancellor Robert Hutchins and late Giuseppe Borgese, and similarly of the world federalists and other groups, belong to this area of political philosophy.[25]

It seems to me that, wherever international relations are taught in universities, there should be some place, some time for study of the philosophy of international relations: of ideologies ("ideisms"), various idea-systems, and their effect on foreign policies. The future might be entirely different from the past and present. It may require entirely new solutions, for which we may find only limited experience in the past. It may require vision and imagination, phantasy, qualities which are rare, and which grow also by exercise and study. In many respects it is a problem of our own ideology.

Mutual Relation of Concepts

Now we may relate our ideological concepts. They are complementary, sometimes overlapping, but above all, their mutual relationship is one of broader concepts and those of narrower within the former. A graph, outlined below (Table IV) may be helpful in relating, organizing concepts of this chapter. Ideas grow in and mirror a culture (first circle). They are part of it and germinate in a culture. Cultural idea-system (second circle) is then a part of a culture. "Cultural idea-system" is a broad concept; it is a concept of an idea system of a whole culture, which can be narrowed down to a definite or less defined political idea-system (third circle), which is a part of it. We usually have more than one political idea system. To simplify our discussion we shall limit our discussion to one. Within the political idea-system, the vision of a world order is conceived, or simply an existing system supported (fourth circle). Within the whole ideology and vision national interest is formulated (fifth circle) while strategic objectives form its core (center). The "doctrine" is a profile, cut through all four concentric circles—as it is a concrete formulation, in which all elements of an ideology might be involved. Ide-

[25] The *World Constitution* was submitted by the Chicago Committee in 1947, published later by Chicago University Press.

ology is influenced by dynamic and changing interests (In_1, In_2, In_3, etc.).

Strategic ideological objectives have to be translated into action; through action ideas are transformed into reality. At least, those who release the action try to translate them into reality. In consequence, tactical objectives are projected from the strategic, and policies are released toward tactical goals. There is not one, but a number of tactical goals (T_1, T_2, T_3, T_4,

TABLE IV

Foreign Policy; Culture—Ideology—Objectives

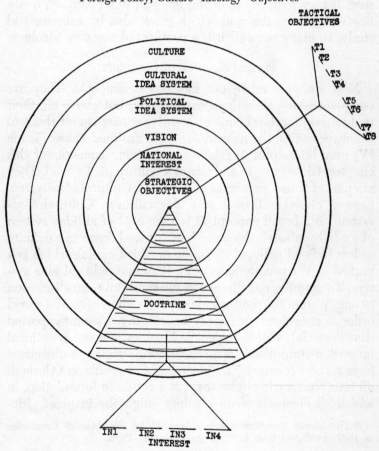

etc.). From tactical objectives the road leads again to materialization of strategic objectives—ends—as outlined in ideology. Strategic goals may never be achieved. Once they are achieved or once a government is close to their achievement the concepts of national interest might be reinterpreted, re-

TABLE V

Political Idea-Systems and Foreign Policy-Objectives of various parties

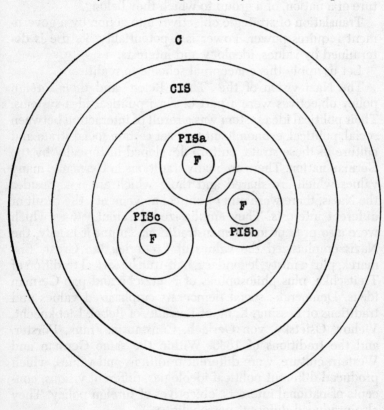

C = Culture

CIS = Cultural Idea Systems

PISa, PISb, PISc = Political Idea Systems of various political parties

F = Foreign Policy Objective

evaluated, new strategic goals might be designed, and, in consequence, new policies released toward new goals.

Some governments, some political parties have a very elaborate ideology, as well as foreign policy ideology. Others may have less elaborate plans. But every culture has a cultural idea-system. A political party may have only a rudimentary program, but still, its members make decisions within an idea-system, which is a part of their personality and a part of culture of a nation, of a group to which they belong.

Translation of strategic objectives into action by a government requires power. Power is a potentiality, its use is determined by values, ideology and interests.

Let us apply this conceptual scheme to realities.

The Nazi vision of the "Third Reich" and their foreign policy objectives were a part of Nazi political idea-systems. Their political idea system was a result of interaction between social, political, economic interests of certain social strata and culture of those strata, culture developed historically by the German nation. There are many traditions in Germany, many values which are shared and those which are not. Besides the Nazis, there were other political movements, the result of different interests. They emphasized different values which were also present in German tradition. To put it briefly, the Nazis emphasized the values of Frederick the Great, Bismarck, plus a misty, legendary, half-true historical tradition of Treitschke, plus philosophies of Nietzsche and pan-German ideas. Democrats, social democrats emphasized values and traditions of Lessing, Kant, of Lassalle, of Bebel, Liebknecht, Vichov, Osietsky, von Gerlach, Constantin Franz, Förster, and the traditions of 1848. Within the same German and Western culture, were different traditions and values, which produced different political ideologies, different visions, concepts of national interests, objectives of foreign policy. They also produced different personalities.

Lenin and Stalin were, of course, products of Russia and Russian culture, and of a broader cultural development involving Europe and Asia. Struggle against the Tsar and the democratic tradition of Russia has produced the political ideologies of the Populists, (later Social-Revolutionaries), democratic Socialists (Mensheviks) and degenerated also in Bolshevik ideology. Within the same culture were different values and traditions, and in consequence different political idea-systems have developed, as well as different concepts of conduct of foreign policy, and of national interest. (Table V)*

* Values of an idea system can be empirically described. In such a quality they are empirical facts. Our personal choices, decisions, however, contain a value judgment (right or wrong) and such a choice, contrary to a description is not empirical but normative. Description of facts might be however influenced by values (see pp. 16 and 88). Professor Florian Znaniecki commented as follows on problems of values as discussed in this book: "A distinction should be made in the domain of social sciences between non-evaluative, *scientific* investigation of human values and the choice and acceptance of certain values for practical reasons.

"This is especially clear in the realm of sociology, but also in economics, linguistics, comparative theory of religions. A sociologist as a scientist investigates both *other people's 'values'*, as empirical 'facts,' without using any evaluative judgments of his own (except the standards and norms of objective scientific research). He introduces his own valuations only when he applies the results of his objective sociological research to the solution of those 'social' (not sociological) problems which he considers important from the practical point of view. The same distinction is found in the domain of natural sciences: a physicist or chemist has to use evaluative judgment only when he functions as an engineer."

As Professor Znaniecki's remarks arrived only after the page proofs had been made, his comments had to be inserted here. I agree entirely with his views and have elaborated this approach in detail in my article mentioned in footnote 4.

CHAPTER V

Factors

The Role of Factors

FACTORS in foreign policy are elements of power, spiritual or material, necessary to enforce a policy and to reach an objective. Factors are either more stable or changing. I am using the adverb "more" as a lastingly stable factor, eternally stable factors do not exist. They all change in history.

It is rather easy to design objectives of foreign politics; it is, however, difficult to enforce policies. The latter requires material and immaterial factors. Without them, they cannot be implemented. A policy of conquest, such as Hitler's, required military strength. To create and to organize a powerful, conquering, striking military machine, it was necessary to build up a national economy geared to the needs of a powerful army. Thus by building his army, Hitler was adjusting the military factors by building a war economy, his economic factor was being adjusted to the objectives of his international politics. Furthermore, a large population was needed for future occupation of vast conquered territories. Hitler's population policy of a high birth rate was also adjusted to the strategic objectives of foreign politics. An emotional element, a mass hysteria, was needed to plunge large masses of German nationals into war. Again Hitler's propaganda and terror machine was building up the German idea system to the same strategic objectives. In this way Hitler built up factors necessary for his strategic objectives: the conquest of Eastern Europe, Russia, Europe, and the world.

Thus the objectives depend strongly on factors. If we design objectives in our foreign policy, we must ask ourselves what are the factors, economic and non-economic elements, which are necessary to enforce such objectives. It might happen that the factors are not satisfactory and that there are no possibilities of building up such factors. If, however, there is a possibility of building up the factors necessary to arrive at the long range goals—strategic objectives—but time is needed to adjust the factors, then usually short range, tactical objectives are chosen, which would provide the time element necessary to develop the factors required for the final ends. That is one of the roles of short range or tactical objectives.

Actual, existing factors in the last analysis are as significant as potentialities of factors. Choice of objectives is related to existing factors or to potentialities but without either one, without power, objectives are irrelevant. Let us imagine that, prior to 1939, a dictatorship—let us say in Estonia—decided to conquer the Soviet Union and establish a greater-Estonian empire. Such objectives could not originate in a healthy mind—even in a mentally healthy extremist mind those objectives could not have been related to the factors. Neither the economic factor of Estonia, nor the military, demographic were present nor could they be created, because of lack of potentialities. A Russian would say—hands are too short.

Factors are not isolated, static, well-defined units. They cannot be studied as isolated, independent phenomena. In the proper factor analysis two principles are essential: mutual interdependence of factors and, what we may call—a context situation.

Factors are mutually, or we may say, functionally related. Understanding of this mutual interdependence, relationship, permits seeing the total, whole picture of the problem-situation, as well as evaluation of weight, significance of single factors. Because of this mutual interdependence, change in one of the factors reacts on the others, involves their readjustment. Adjustment of factors in turn releases social processes, which affect the complex canvas of human society. European integration had its effective expression in the Schuman Plan—the coal and steel community of Europe. According to this plan, coal and iron freely circulate within the member states of the community and tariff walls for both have been abolished. Today, the Plan works with a number of limitations; it still works however. The Schuman Plan was a change of an economic factor in Europe's international politics. It has affected other factors—such as the political factor—(Council of Europe), as well as trends towards further political integration. It creates conditions for a European Defense Community. It affects political program of parties, policies of trade unions, wages and general conditions of workers, price levels of coal and iron, movement of labor, transport, commercial policy, the whole production. Change of one factor in European international economics has forced a chain process of readjustment of other factors; and released interacting social processes.

Change or adjustment of factors is a subject of an empirical study. It is not an abstraction. Factors are rooted in, they are a part of a concrete problem situation. Stalin's expansionist policy involved readjustment of a number of factors in the Soviet Union. His policy produced a reaction—Western democracies had to readjust their policies and factors to the dangers of aggression. Here is a complex problem-situation —a reality, with a number of factors. The latter can be studied, analyzed *in relation*, in the context of a definite situation. Such an approach we shall call a context-situation. This term is borrowed from linguistics and anthropology. Anthropologist Bronislaw Malinowski argued that words, symbols can be properly understood only in their "context-situation" —an utterance has to be related to a situation in which it has been pronounced. Symbols, utterances, detached from culture, reality, situation, he argued, cannot be properly understood. Utterances describing pearl-fishing in the South Seas can be understood by an outsider only if the whole process of pearl-fishing—unknown to us—is described and utterances explained with their function.[26] Factors in international rela-

[26] C. K. Ogden, J. A. Richards, *The Meaning of Meaning*, with supplementary Essays by B. Malinowski and F. G. Crookshank, London, 1936, p. 306.

tions become a useful tool of analysis, not as farfetched abstractions, but as properly related to the whole, concrete situation, to the context-situation. Thus, factor is an elastic concept—a concept which has to be adjusted, changed to fit a given historical and concrete situation.

Therefore, it is hardly possible to specify a precise number of factors of foreign policy. Morgenthau (op. cit. pp. 80–105) suggests eight factors ("elements of national power"): 1) geography; 2) national resources; 3) industrial capacity; 4) military preparedness; 5) population; 6) national character; 7) national morale; 8) the quality of diplomacy.

Analysis of a specific policy, or of a specific situation may require a different emphasis on various factors; also new factors may emerge. With this in mind we may suggest a working proposition of the following factors: 1) geographical; 2) economic; 3) demographic; 4) military; 5) social-political; 6) culture and social-psychological; 7) leadership, diplomacy.

Some factors are partially overlapping—or parts of larger concepts. Manpower is also an economic problem. However population, its number, dynamics, growth or decline, is essential in an analysis as a specific factor, as much as it is important as a part of the economic. In social sciences overlapping of concepts is hardly avoidable.

Geographic Factor

The geographical factor, a relatively stable one, was one of the most discussed factors of foreign policy. Analysis of the geographical factor became a "cause celèbre" of international relations. Geographers and men of politics for almost a century made of it a cornerstone of international politics. Among many theorists, Alfred Thayer Mahan and Sir Halford J. Mackinder have won fame and influence in Anglo-American politics and scholarship. Both influenced decisively German geopolitics; their theories became also important in German military thought. Mahan's ideas influenced the Emperor William, while Mackinder's influence was decisive on Haushoffer, the great master and medicine man of Ger-

man "Geopolitik." Haushoffer, a teacher of Hess, is credited
with direct influence on Adolf Hitler and his strategy.

Mahan's thesis could be digested into a formula: "He who
governs water—governs the land-mass"; "he who governs
oceans—governs the continent." The Mackinder theory was a
reverse one: "He who controls land—controls water"; "he who
controls continents—controls the oceans."

Mahan, the father of imperial navalism, took his inspira-
tion from the British navalism and colonialism. Commerce
and colonies are a prerequisite of prosperity and national
greatness—both need a navy. The Mackinder theory does not
deny the significance of the sea masses. The control of the sea
masses, however, is determined by the control of land masses;
the land base, as a center of production and supply, is instrumental in development of a naval potential and support of
naval operations. The base decides about strength and security of the navy. What will happen if the Great Continent—
Eurasia—"World Island" as Mackinder calls it—or even only
a large part of it—should come under control of one single
power? What will happen, asks Mackinder, if such a land
mass becomes a "single base?" The other "insular" bases, like
Great Britain won't be able to balance such a power with
ships and manpower. They will fight—certainly with heroism,
inherited through history—but their fate will be sealed. Such
development of world politics which will lead to the creation
of such a continental base is a threat to the world's liberty,
answers Sir Halford. Those views, expressed back in 1919
(the book was reissued in 1942) in his "Democratic Ideals and
Reality" were certainly prophetic. The war spread to the
shores of the United States, once Germany conquered parts
of the Great Continent. Today the dangers of world war and
conflicts reappeared when the Soviet Union extended its control over large parts of the continent, almost to the suburbs
of the Atlantic and Mediterranean. Even more prophetic was
Mackinder in 1904, fifty years ago in his lecture on the "Geographical Pivot of History" at the Royal Geographic Society
in London, where he seemed rather to startle the audience
with his thesis that the pivot of history is the land masses of

Asia—and that future centuries will develop even more
around these vast areas. Speaking of Russia, he argued that
Russia took the place of the Mongol Empire, and her pressure
on its neighbors substitutes for the raids of the steppemen.
"Nor is it likely that any possible social revolution will alter
her essential relations to the great geographical limits of her
existence . . ." What may happen in case Russia should ally
herself with Germany? ". . . The threat of such an event
should, therefore, throw France into alliance with the over-
sea powers, and France, Italy, Egypt, India, and Korea would
become so many bridgeheads where the outside navies would
support armies to compel the pivot allies to deploy land
forces and prevent them from concentrating their whole
strength on fleets."[27] In 1954 we may replace the word "alliance" by control—Soviet control over East Germany and
satellite countries—and in consequence we have a Korean
landing, which Mackinder foresaw fifty years ago!

Impressive as this is, still Mackinder, especially in his
early views, represents a deterministic approach. His writings
—brilliant, intelligent, penetrating, still leave an impression
that geography determines the fate of men and history. The
"strategical opportunities," argues Sir Halford, are uneven;
so is the fertility and wealth of the land on which nations are
growing. Nations have an uneven opportunity and here is
one reason for struggle. "Unless I wholly misread the facts of
geography, I would go further, and say that the groupings
of lands and seas, and of fertility and natural pathways, is
such as to lend itself to the growth of empires, and in the
end of a single world-empire."[28]

Geography by itself (with possible rare exceptions) does
not determine the fate of human society. There is a continuous interaction between man and his environment; the geographic environment is influenced by man. Man's influence
over his environment depends strongly upon his social or-

[27] From an Address by H. J. Mackinder reported in the *National Geographic Magazine* for Aug. 1904, pp. 331–335.
[28] Halford Mackinder: *Democratic Ideas and Reality*, Henry Holt Co.,
1942, p. 2.

ganization and technology. Of course a primitive group is under strong pressure of geographic environment. Salination of water, as Ellsworth Huntington discovered in Central Asia ("Pulse of Asia") forced whole populations out of old cities. Modern technology, however, changes not only the landscape, but even the significance of certain areas, the significance of present geographic distribution. Technology is a product of man. The human factor, and we may observe it whenever man acts, is powerful and significant. In times of Mackinder, the Arctic did not play any strategic role. After the second World War the polar region became of primary significance. The political significance of geographic distribution of certain areas has definitely changed in our century.

The invention of the airplane has changed our geographical outlook. Maps provide a generation with a compass and orientation in international politics. Maps mirror man's understanding, man's views of the planet. The maps of Columbus and our maps are mirrors of a world outlook of two different generations. Mercator's projection—a projection in which we clearly distinguish America, Europe, Asia, Africa, Australia—was the map on which generations since the great discoveries, including ourselves, were raised. Today, the new generations are raised with another map—the Arctic projection, world projection focussed on the Arctic. The seal of the League of Nations had a Mercator's projection of the world. The United Nations seal is an Arctic projection. The League of Nations seal reflected the seaman's and landman's viewpoint and outlook. The United Nations seal represents an airman's outlook. Our outlook of the globe has changed, because of our technology; so did the strategy. In Mackinder's theory, Eastern Europe is the key in the strategy of the Great Continent. It was his axiom that who rules East Europe controls the "heartland," the great land mass, and control of the heartland is the key to control of the world. No doubt, Eastern Europe today plays a vital role in world politics. Occupation of Eastern Europe by the Soviet Union has put the Western democracies into a situation of permanent danger. Europe was reduced to a peninsula but today in world strategy, the Arctic area plays a vital, important role, while it did not play any role fifty years ago, back in 1904, when Mackinder presented his paper. In February 1949 (weekly of Feb. 11–17) the Paris paper *Le Monde* in a leading article "La strategie du B-36" indicated the significance of the Arctic in global strategy and global foreign policy. New types of flying machines were changing history and geography. A map of the world from the vantage of the Arctic was a lucid illustration to an editorial viewpoint. On March 20, 1949, the *New York Times* in an article (signed H.W.B.) entitled "The Polar Regions Assume a New Strategic Importance" emphasized the significance of the Arctic in world politics. The writer explained the "polar concept" . . . the polar ice caps ceased to be a barrier. We have to give justice to the Royal Geographical Society. At the Mackinder meeting Amery argued against his thesis. He predicted that the airplane would change the distribution of significant geographic areas. It was back in 1904, in times of Kitty Hawk, Blériot, and the Wright brothers, in times when cavalry, not tanks, was paramount, and there were still more kings than those in cards on the thrones of Europe.

Technology, aeronautics, created by man, has, in consequence, changed the geographic factor. Stable as the latter is, it is still dynamic because human society is dynamic and geography in our approach is significant in its relation to men and society. But technology is not the only variable which influences the geographic factor. Geographic environment is similar to a tool; man's skills and values will determine its use. It can be used for war or peace. The Danube could be an avenue of conquest—in our times, it was more an artery of trade. The Mediterranean was used for conquest by aggressive tribes and nations, but the Mediterranean was also an important means of communication through which culture was diffused, and Judeo-Christian ethics spread. Culture and values of nations have changed; so has the international significance of certain geographical areas. Norwegians, Swedes were a nation of warriors. For centuries Vikings from Scandinavia raided the continent to its western and eastern corners, and conquered nations, gathered spoils, founded states. So did the Swedes. In the museums of Stockholm there is an impressive collection of foreign flags, taken by Swedes on the continent. Charles XII was probably the last of the great conquerors, who led his army southeast toward the steppe-land. After he was killed, Sweden began to turn toward goals which were closer to Swiss than to Viking tradition. What happened—that a nation of Scandinavian warriors became one of the most peaceful, constructive nations of Europe? It was culture values, personalities, historical experiences, change in social economic structure—in brief the human factor, which has contributed to this change. With it the "geopolitical significance" of the Scandinavian peninsula has changed. Sweden, instead of a dagger of Europe, became an outskirt, far beyond the reach of great European political hurricanes.

Geographical areas play a different role in different periods of world history. However, if an aggressive group seizes power over a nation, and the policy of state becomes expansionist, then, of course, geographical areas play a vital strategic role in a policy of expansion. An aggressive government in Germany and Russia may form a dangerous combination, an alliance for conquest. Then, of course, their control of "heartland" and Eastern Europe becomes a mortal danger for Western democracies. Creation of a European unity may affect values and loyalties of German youth, and when attitudes of a nation change significance of certain areas which were once bases for aggression, may change too. Mackinder's anticipations were so startlingly true. Both nations—Germany and Russia—came in our times under the control of powerful expansionist groups. For years to come, Mackinder's theory may remain a warning because attitudes and values change slowly, very slowly; sometimes it takes generations.

The geographical factor, being relatively stable, should be analyzed within a sociological and political context. The geographical factor in foreign politics is not an isolated factor, it is not a sole determinant of power. For practical politics, however, let us not forget that cultural patterns, attitudes, and nations change very slowly, and therefore "national psychology" or "cultural pattern" for working purposes, for a working analysis may be accepted as relatively stable too. Great shock, catastrophe, which affects the whole nation—as Nazi occupation and Soviet occupation of Eastern Europe did—may result however in sudden change, similar to unique, traumatic experience in personality formation of an individual. Such a change will be reflected in geopolitics, as geopolitics is manmade.

Economic Factor

Discussion of the geographical factor already indicated the significance of the "human" factor, the continuous interaction between material environment on one hand and an individual, human society, culture, on the other. Machines, wealth, are manmade, too. They may be used by him for war or for peace.

The economic factor is not identical with a purely "material" accumulation of capital or raw materials. The Swiss with a beautiful countryside, but hardly rich in soil or raw materials, have developed a considerable industry, finances—economic potential. The Iranians with very rich oil deposits are a society of low capital income—a poorhouse with a large staff of wealthy, sometimes fabulously wealthy overseers.

The elements of the economic factor are rather complex; still, as a working proposition, they have to be reduced to a more simple formula. Raw materials, capital accumulation, and the human factor form its important elements. The human factor is again a fundamental one. The abilities, talents, skills, energy, vitality, of a people are instrumental in proper use of its potentialities. "An Atomic Map of the World" published by the *New York Times* (October 11, 1953) might be a proper illustration. This map contains: 1) major production centers; 2) major deposits of fissionable materials and; 3) research centers, among others. In other words, we have here three elements: accumulation of capital in form of production potentialities, raw materials and the human factor. Manpower is a part of the human factor. It is an important one.

Manpower, however, alone, without its relationship to the raw materials, capital accumulation, its skills, training, explains little.

Probably steel might be today the single index best adopted for study of potentials in foreign policy analysis. The steel production, the whole volume of consumption and per capita consumption, may be a good index of economic po-

TABLE VI

Steel Potential[29]

	Luxemburg 1948	China 1948	Manchuria 1945	India 1948
Production of Crude Steel in 1000 Metric Tons	2453	10**	900***	1200**
	census 1947	estimates 1951		census 1951
Population	286,786	463,500,000		356,829,485

** U.N. Secretariat estimates
*** Manchuria's crude steel production

1945	1946	1947	1948	1952–3
900	40†	20†		20‡

† secretariat estimates
‡ secretariat estimated maximum attainable production

tential. This index may sometimes hide quite a surprise; Luxemburg becomes a giant and China a dwarf—Luxemburg with population below 300 thousand and a steel production more than twice as large as that of India with a population of over 350 millions, and 2½ times as large as that of China and Manchuria with a population of almost half a billion, is still a tiny European country. Luxemburg manpower is insignificant but its economic potential is high. Economic potential is not the sole factor in foreign politics. The economic potential is

[29] Compiled from *European Steel Trends in the Setting of the World Markets*, United Nations, Steel Division, Economic Commission for Europe, Geneva, 1949, and *U.N. Demographic Yearbook 1952*.

not an "isolate" and should be always compared with other
factors. Our comparison indicates the weakness of China's
economic potential. However, manpower counts, and contributes to the role of China in foreign policy. Imports of steel
from the U.S.S.R. and satellite countries may increase China's
war potential to a highly dangerous point—as we learned in
Korea. Still, study of steel may indicate that China's modern
war potential is entirely dependent upon foreign sources.
Simple data on Chinese steel production gives us understanding of the Achillean weakness of Chinese communist imperialism. Production of Manchuria only partially changes this
picture. Estimates of the U.N. indicate that in the coming
years the whole picture will change little.

TABLE VII

Production of Coal, Steel, and Electricity[30]

	1913	1929	1937	1951
Hard coal (millions of tons)				
Western Europe	499	511	492	478
Eastern Europe	79	97	88	105
U.S.S.R.	30	37	109	225
United States	517	550	448	519[a]
Steel (millions of tons)				
Western Europe	35	48	50	58
Eastern Europe	5	6	6	10
U.S.S.R.	4	5	18	31
United States	32	57	51	95
Electricity[b] (billions of kwh)				
Western Europe	—	89	132	274
Eastern Europe	—	19	29	50
U.S.S.R.	—	6	36	103
United States	—	92	119	370

Note: All data refer to present boundaries.
[a] Including a small amount of lignite.
[b] Including production outside public utilities, except for the United Kingdom and the United States.

[30] Source: *United Nations, Economic Survey of Europe Since the War*,
a Reappraisal of Problems and Prospects, Prepared by the Research and
Planning Division Economic Commission for Europe, Geneva, 1953, p.
197.

For Europe and America more complete figures are available. Comparison of U.N. figures of: population, net output of industry, steel consumption, average annual net output of industry per head, average annual consumption of steel per head, may supply an "economic compass" in foreign policy analysis.

TABLE VIII
Steel Potential[31]

Country	Population (*in millions*)		Net output of industry (*in thousand millions of dollars at 1936 prices*)		Steel consumption (*in millions of tons*)	
	1947	1948	1947	1948	1947	1948
Austria	6.9	7.0	0.19	0.30	0.3	0.5
Belgium-Luxemburg	8.7	8.8	0.88	0.96	1.9	2.2
Czechoslovakia	12.2	12.3	0.76	0.89	2.0	2.4
France	41.3	41.8	3.00	3.41	6.2	7.6
Italy	45.5	46.0	1.46	1.56	1.9	2.4
Poland	23.5	24.0	0.74	0.95	1.6	1.7
Sweden	6.8	6.9	1.06	1.10	2.0	2.0
United Kingdom	49.6	50.0	7.23	8.10	11.6	13.5

Comparison of our demographic data and steel data may give some interesting indications. Thus far, nations of a higher birth rate have a lower steel potential than countries of a low birth rate, countries of stationary populations. Steel is an index of industrialization. Industrialization, as it is commonly known, affects the birth rate. It lowers both the birth rate and death rate. Thus manpower potential of Asia is counterbalanced by the industrial potential of the United States and Western Europe.

Oil, of course, today, as well as uranium, is important as part of the economic factor. Again, oil not alone, not per se, not without the human factor, not without the interrelationship to other economic, industrial elements. Oil in Iran is an important foreign policy factor. By itself it does not make Iran a first class power. In any foreign policy, however, in a

[31] Source: United Nations, Department of Economic Affairs, *European Steel Trends*, Steel Division, Economic Commission for Europe, Geneva, 1949, pp. 106–7.

policy for world reconstruction and development, for peace—
or in designs for conquest, oil is of paramount significance;
so is Iran. The loss of Iran's oil as a result of Anglo-Iranian
dispute, has immediately affected Western policies, and also
influenced production of oil in other centers. A change in
economic factor of Great Britain has followed.

Country	Average annual net output of industry per head (*in 1938 dollars*)	Average annual consumption of steel per head (*in kilogrammes*)
Austria	35.1	57.6
Belgium-Luxemburg	104.9	234.3
Czechoslovakia	67.5	179.6
France	77.1	166.1
Italy	33.0	47.0
Poland	35.5	69.5
Sweden	158.1	292.0
United Kingdom	154.0	252.0

Industrial capacity of a country and abilities, industrial
knowledge of a nation are significant factors; they may balance the power of others derived from control of vital geographical areas, such as large land masses, and also its demo-
graphical element, the manpower. The scientific research,
know-how talents became a true factor, or a part of industrial
factors.[31a]

Scientific abilities are again a factor, or a part of a factor,
in a policy oriented for cooperation or for conflict. Nuclear
power and the whole atom industry is of course of primary

[31a] Drew Middleton in *Britain Cut Units Abroad Build Mobile Force at
Home, New York Times*, January 28, 1954, reports that changes in British
defense plans are due to the following facts: ". . . that the immediate danger
of war with the Soviet Union had receded steadily in the last year and that
the time had come to replan defense in anticipation of a considerable period
of uneasy balance between East and West. During this period, when the
weight of manpower will be on the side of the Russo-Chinese alliance, these
sources said, it will be of primary importance to further the West's lead in
scientific weapons."

Earl Alexander emphasized that in designing a defense program Britain
must look years ahead and "try to visualize the pattern of war which will
result from the new weapons which our scientists invent or are set to
develop."

significance in times when the world can be divided into atomic and non-atomic powers, into countries which control what amounts to an atomic industry, and those who do not. However, at present only countries with a great industrial potential can develop the A or H bomb. Industrial potential can be measured in terms of steel better than in terms of atom, as data are available and more explanatory.

In a long range analysis, steel as an index has its specific qualities. In a foreign policy of mutual aid with technical assistance, in any long range policy oriented toward peace, cooperation and world organisation, steel is a far better index than, for instance, nuclear power. Thus far, in this stage of technological development, the emphasis in the advancement of nuclear power is rather on its destructive quality, while steel is multivalent,—as the same emphasis, if not greater is on its constructive uses. It played a primary role in the development of our modern industrial civilization, in the advancement of standards of living, sanitation, comfort, transport and housing. Even countries of high agricultural yields, have also a high per capita consumption of steel such as the United States, Great Britain, the Scandinavian countries, Canada. Therefore, steel is a factor of importance in an analysis of a constructive foreign policy.

Population Factor

From the viewpoint of foreign policy, we may regard the demographic factor as static in a short-range approach, dynamic and changing in a long-range approach. However, the dynamic character of population change also influences the short-range objectives. Nations with a rising birth rate might have a different policy, and might undertake different risks than a nation with a declining birth rate.

States may be divided into large, medium and small *in population;* what a "large" and what a "small" state is, can be rather answered in terms of experience than in terms of definitions and definite numbers. States like the United States, India, and China are usually regarded as "large" in population. Here are a few examples: large: United States with a population of 153,692,811 (census 1950); U.S.S.R., 201,300,-000 (census 1950, figures estimated); India, 337,211,000 (census 1948, figures estimated); medium-size population: Poland with an estimated population of about 24,160,000 (1949); Rumania with over 15,872,000; nations of small populations: Albania, 1,175,000 (estimated); Denmark, 4,251,500.

The population factor should be analyzed in its mutual relationship with other factors. The size of population should not be confused with power. A state with less population but with a better balanced economy, more political consensus, with voluntary cooperation of its citizens, and more united in an approval, support, of a way of life they cherish, might be stronger than a nation or state of far larger population. The population of China or India is larger than that of the United States. Still, the United States, as a power in a situation either of conflict or cooperation, is stronger. The United States feeds the world, while the latter are areas of repetitive famines. The potential power of states is expressed in a combination of factors and their mutual relationship, never in a single factor, such as population.

The cultural pattern, not solely the quantity of population is, in certain situations of paramount significance. The technical assistance program, point 4, might be a good illustration here. A small-size nation, with a large percentage of highly skilled workers, well trained technicians, medical men and social scientists, might be a "big power," in the best sense, for peace and cooperation—in helping an underdeveloped large-size population state, such as China, in technical, agricultural, and social advancement. Similarly, in a conflict-oriented situation, "quality" of population, its training, skills in developing an industrial potential, economic factor are of relevance.

Once all other factors or at least some of them, aside from population, are similar, then a comparative analysis, based on population size, is even more relevant. To use this formula *ceteris paribus*, we may compare Western European powers—such as Belgium, France, Sweden. In such comparison population size plays a more relevant role, as factor of strength,

than does comparison of two powers of uneven population
and different economic, geographic, and other potentials. In
the latter case, the population size has to be related to resources, industrial potential, quality of population, and eventually other factors.

The population must always be related to a situation. In
certain situations it plays a major decisive role; in others a
lesser one. In times of biological extermination, population
factor played a very significant one.

For the first time in modern times, during the Second
World War, some nations of Europe were faced with the
problem of biological survival. Some were given a choice,
some none. The leadership of the Polish underground, Council of National Unity, never considered any "choice" between
collaboration and struggle. Struggle was their policy—en-
slavement, biological destruction, Hitler's. The Jews of Poland were faced with a most brutal situation. No choice of
biological survival was given to them by the Germans: death
as slaves, death in subservience or death as free men—death
in a mortal fight against the overwhelming German and Quis-
ling troops. Underground leadership of the Jewish people in
Warsaw chose the latter. The Norwegians had a choice, as
Hitler was willing to accept them as allies. Most of them,
however, answered with their moral support for the resistance. The Serbian people were in jeopardy similar to that
of the Poles. The Soviet government applied different methods in many areas from the Baltic to the Balkans, such as
mass deportation and "liquidation" of national leadership.
Both Nazi Germany and the Communist Soviet Union built a
social and material machinery of mass extermination and deportation, a proposition which was and still is "colossal." For
the first time in history the factory system, concepts of mass
production were projected into mass destruction of men by
Hitler. As Hitler was the inventor of murder on the "assembly
line," so was Stalin the inventor of mass deportation by the
use of modern transportation techniques. Stalin, a true Gen-
ghis Khan with a telephone, employed engines and tele-
phones to make swift decisions about forced mass move-

ments. Both seemed to have made an important contribution to the thesis that scientific advance, technological advance is "neutral," "instrumental," per se—it may be used for good or evil.

In such situations, national committees or governments-in-exile of nations overrun by those organizations of mass destruction and mass deportation, had to make decisions about types of struggle or types of submission. A small nation of 1½–2 millions, such as the Baltic countries, can be wiped off the map today in the course of a few years. A medium size nation like Poland may undertake a resistance for a certain period, as its size will give better chances of biological survival.

To sum up—if, in theory, the population factor alone would decide in such situations, a nation of two millions, if surrounded by very populous nations led by an aggressive government could not for the sake of survival, undertake the same actions as a nation of, let us say, twenty millions. Under the modern policy of warfare and conquest, Nazi and Soviet mass deportations, concentration camps, and mass execution, a nation of two millions may rather easily be physically destroyed. Problems of biological survival may contribute to a certain behavior pattern as well as to the foreign policy of a small nation, which a powerful nation may reject. However, such is a situation in *theory, if solely* the population factor would decide. Thus far, the population factor alone was not the only one as a premise of a policy decision. The values of the members of the government and value of the national culture play a significant role. The government of small Finland, when threatened by the Soviet government in 1940, chose armed defense and war, rejected a surrender. However, after the experience of the second World War, such as mass extermination, the weight of population factor may grow in policy decision, at those most tragic moments of nations and of men.

Population, in the long range, is a continuously changing dynamic factor. Today in Europe alone there are more people than there were in the whole world before 1650. In 1939

Europe had 540 millions. In the middle of the XVII century
Europe had one-fifth of it—about 100 millions. Since 1800
Europe's population increased three times; since 1850 it had
doubled.[32] In the early XVIII century the most populous
country of Europe was France. Russia passed France in
the XVIII century, Germany passed France about 1870, Italy
about 1930.[33]

A change in the population factor can be anticipated; this
was done by the League of Nations project headed by Prof.
Notenstein. The analysis of trends 1940–1970 in Europe and
the Soviet Union indicated roughly an increase of population

TABLE IX

Of the Total Population of Europe (= 100)
The Proportion in Each Country in the Year[34]

	1880	1910
England and Wales	7.77	8.06
Scotland	1.12	1.06
Ireland	1.55	0.98
France	11.20	8.76
Germany	13.54	14.52
Austria	6.63	6.38
Belgium	1.65	1.66
Hungary	4.71	4.67
Italy	8.52	7.75
Russia	25.82	29.13
All other countries	17.49	17.03

in Southeastern Europe and Russia, decrease in Western Europe. However, actual later U.N. figures, based on a census,
indicated a significant discrepancy between the figures anticipated by Professor Notenstein for Western Europe, and the
actual reproduction rates. Western Europe did better in

[32] *The Future Population of Europe and the Soviet Union, Populations Projections, 1940–1970,* by Frank Notenstein, Irene B. Taeuber,
Dudley Kirk, Ansley J. Coale, Louise K. Kiser, of the Office of Population Research, Princeton University, League of Nations, Geneva, 1944,
p. 44.

[33] op. cit., p. 62.

[34] Carr-Saunders, A. M., *Population,* (Chapter: Population and International Relations) Oxford University Press, 1925, 1931, p. 77. Quoted
from, S. Newsholme., *The Elements of Vital Statistics,* Allen, Unwin,
1923, p. 54.

birth-rate than was anticipated by Notenstein. Whether the trend in Western Europe is a lasting one, is hard to predict.[35]

The difference in culture is also reflected in the dynamic aspect, in population growth, especially in reproduction and death rates. Difference in culture is often difference in nationality. Overpopulation of certain areas may at most contribute to expansionist, warlike policies; however, overpopulation per se does not cause wars. Here, too, the population problem has to be considered within the whole cultural context, it has to be related to values. Again we may quote here differences in foreign policies of an overpopulated India of Nehru's government, and overpopulated Japan, under a militaristic rule.

The Military Factor

Both the actual and potential strength of the military factors are evaluated and related to other factors, as well as to the problem situation.

In times of Napoleon, the standing army, at a given moment, was a pretty accurate index of a country's war poten-

[35] Population science has made great advances in recent times. Analysis of the population factor in foreign policy requires knowledge of basic demographic concepts, such as differential reproduction rates and the differential growth of population. The three types of population classes, as defined by Warren S. Thompson: pre-industrial, expanding, stationary, are helpful in general analysis of trends. Important studies on population factors in international politics have been made, to mention as examples: Warren S. Thompson, *Population and Peace in the Pacific,* University of Chicago Press, 1945, basic study of Prof. Notenstein and his associates (quoted above), Dudley Kirk's *Europe's Population in the Interwar Years,* League of Nations 1946, Frank Lorimer's *The Population of the Soviet Union, History and Prospects,* League of Nations, 1946, and many others. In some general books on population, international problems connected with population are discussed extensively as in A. M. Carr-Saunders, *Population,* Oxford University Press, 1925, and in other works of the same author, who is one of the world's leading demographers. Publications of the United Nations Statistical Office, such as *Population Index, Statistical Yearbook,* supply excellent comparative source-material, though veracity of data—officially supplied—is uneven. The figures of the Communist-controlled and other totalitarian countries are highly questionable. Space and scope of this study does not permit discussion of methods of analysis of population changes, from the viewpoint of foreign policy and international relations.

tial. Not any more. A country with a small standing army—as
the United States in 1914 or 1938—may have a tremendous
military potential, while a country with a relatively large
one, as China, may have a far lower military potential.
Distinction between existing, actual and potential military
power, military factor is today relevant; discrepancies between both are far greater than in the times of Bonaparte.

Potential is measured by the industrial capacity of a country, by its spiritual strength, social, economic, political stability, control of relevant geographic areas. The actual military
establishment by itself alone is not any more the sole index.
Infantry is not any more the queen of the army. Cruel as it
is, in the second half of the XX century, the powers could be
divided into atomic and non-atomic powers. Maybe this division, brutal as it is, was in the time of the cold war the most
convincing. Churchill argued at certain times of Soviet
high-pressure that peace hangs on atomic supremacy of the
United States. Once the secret was stolen, and forwarded to
the Soviet agencies war dangers increased. Actions of American statesmen are controlled by public opinion, by moral restraints, by philosophy of power, rooted in moderation and
balance. The Soviet leaders, with their philosophy of naked
power without moral restraint, represent a different risk.
Atom secrets in their hands are a different proposition than in
the hands of American statesmen. Power does not equate
with power like two and two. The same amount of power in
American hands is a different proposition from the same
amount of power in Soviet hands. Here fail the philosophers
of power in international relations, who reduce everything
to an equation $x =$ power.

The weight of the military potential shifts to non-military
aspects— such as industrial capacity, scientific research, moral
factors. Even the very character of armed forces has changed.
Armies of illiterate recruits, long hours of marching, belong
to the past. The American Air-force is in reality an army of
officers. On a plane, in actual combat, the element of cooperation seems to be more significant than the elements of subor-
dination. The deep cleavage between officers and soldiers, ac-

cented since centuries in uniform, has disappeared in this external expression—clothing. In the American Air Force, soldiers, non-coms, officers are dressed the same way in combat, their clothing is that of factory workers. Outside the service clothing of officers and non-officers is almost the same and far closer to civilian than ever before.

Counting numbers of divisions, soldiers, hardly may give a *full* picture of the military factor, though manpower has its significance and should not be underestimated. Even figures of military equipment such as airplanes are not sufficient. The estimates are far more complex: airbases, planes in operation, annual plane production, air force manpower.

This new type of military factor is relevant in a policy of conquest or defense as much as in a policy oriented toward a new vision, toward a vision of mankind organized for peace and constructive cooperation. In the latter case, certain types of industrial activities also represent military potential, and a potential war risk and danger. A country oriented toward peace is willing to accept effective obligations which would prevent the use of such industries for warlike purposes. The Baruch Plan of atomic control might be an example of a peace-oriented policy toward a military-industrial factor.

The military factor, as much as military decisions cannot be separated any longer from political decision. Separation of military courses of action from political, during the second World War was disastrous for the Western powers. This policy permitted Stalin to extend Soviet influence. John J. McCloy, former Assistant-Secretary of War and U. S. High Commissioner, is among the first to indicate inadequacy of a foreign policy which, in times of a great crisis, is based on a principle that military operation and foreign policy are two distinct propositions, which should not be mixed.[36] Harry D. Gideonse, reviewing McCloy's book, wrote, "Our constitutional separation of *function* has led to separation of *thought* so great that we seem to believe that policy should end when

[36] John J. McCloy, *The Challenge to American Foreign Policy*, Harvard U. Press, 1953, and also a penetrating review of this book in *New Leader*, August 3, 1953, by Harry D. Gideonse.

the use of power begins." Of course, supremacy of civilian authority over military, as well as separation of function, is paramount in a democracy. McCloy's and Gideonse's viewpoint emphasizes even more the fact that the military is only one factor, one element of a whole social process of a public policy. Similarly, an analyst should see the totality of this social process. His evaluation of the military factor should indicate clearly that he deals with only a part, with one variable within a social process of closely interrelated factors.

One of those factors of great relevance, but difficult to evaluate, is the military and civilian leadership of the military establishment. Leadership is a paramount element of strength. Similarly, other social, psychological elements—such as army morale, ideology, training—belong to the analysis of this factor, in the sense discussed before.

Social-Political Factor

During the first World War tsarist Russia was a weak country. Its political system based on autocracy made it weak. Revolutionary tensions were strong, government inept; its members did not understand the real social and political conditions within the country. Military defeat, economic difficulties easily released the latent revolutionary forces. In the midst of the war the great colossus collapsed. Iran today is a weak country, in spite of its oil wealth. Distribution of national income is uneven. It is a country of tremendous wealth and luxury on the one hand and misery on the other. On top of an oriental social structure, a Western constitution and parliament is superimposed. A wide discrepancy in per capita income, discrepancy between wealth of few and want of many is a source of considerable weakness in international politics. Lack of an adequate, even fundamental program of great social change, a change which would contribute to greater economic equality and justice, gives in Iran an excellent opportunity to the Communist propaganda. Communist ideology has an appeal to certain social strata of Iran—to the dissatisfied intellectuals. This gives the Communists a fertile ground for establishment of a party apparatus directed against the present rule.

The social and political conditions within a country form an important factor of foreign policy. Standard of living, distribution of income, social structure related to the facts of production and consumption are elements of social strength or weakness, while political institutions, civil rights, political stability, provisions for a peaceful social and political change, are measures of political vigor. Both are closely interwoven. It is comforting that freedom and social justice are symptoms of strength in international politics. It is not accidental that democracies, Scandinavian countries, Great Britain, United States of America, have the highest standard of living, and vice versa, the countries of the highest standard of living are democratic. There is a definite interdependence between both variables.

Masses may be swayed by irrational ideologies and charismatic leaders—as was the case in Nazi Germany. Therefore, not institutions alone, but institutional behavior is relevant. In the Weimar Republic attitudes towards democracy, patterns of political behavior, political mores, were different than those of the British. The leaders of the Weimar Republic could not change overnight patterns of political behavior, produced by generations.

Democratic and non-democratic way of life is mirrored in institutional behavior, behavior within the institutional framework, attitudes toward institutions, and techniques of adjustments. Even between democratic countries there are significant differences in that respect. To compare France and Great Britain, after this war, the political system of France did not provide a framework for both stability and peaceful change. In spite of the strength of progressive social movements, social stratification of France is unhealthy. Few have much and many have little. British adjustment during and after the war was quite different. Political institutions work there very well and the pattern of political behavior provides for their adjustment and necessary institutional changes. Of course the war has affected Britain's economic position.

Thanks to social-economic changes, very many who had less, have more and those who had very much have much less. Great Britain retained its social-economic strength and balance, which most unfortunately, France had not yet achieved. Similarly, political strength of the United States does not rest solely on its military establishment or even industrial capacity. A map of home ownership spreads in the United States (published in the *New York Times*, September 27, 1953) as well as Dr. Simon Kuznets' findings give some element of social strength. The former indicates that in many states over 60% of families live in their own homes. Professor Kuznets' figures (in *"Shares of Upper Income Groups in Income and Savings,"* also *New York Times* article and charts, May 4, 1953) indicate a trend toward increase of a more equalitarian distribution of per capita income in the United States in favor of the lower income groups. Even distribution of income, and widespread relative economic security, reflected in savings of various types, are important factors of American social and political stability, and provide a basis for a system where social change can be effective and nonviolent.

An analysis of foreign policy of a country, of its strength, cannot overlook this point. A country with many infantry regiments and many discontented citizens might be weak, and a country with few regiments, but many loyal and happy citizens, strong. Even a private bank might be a far better risk to invest in a socialist Sweden, than in a pre-capitalist, half-feudal Iran. In the former, social-political factor indicates stability—in the latter, instability. Social-political factor is a measure of a country's moral strength or weakness.

The political factor of foreign policy is also significant in terms of the decision-making process and responsibilities. The political system of a country determines powers and focus and mechanism of decision in foreign policy. The mechanism of decision-making in a democracy is different than in a dictatorship. Those differences are of major significance. The fact that in a dictatorship a foreign policy decision is made secretly, without controls and restraint, contributes to speed of decision and provides the totalitarians with the initial advantage of surprise. In a democracy, foreign policy decisions are made as a part of public, parliamentary debate; their enforcement is slower and subject to moral restraints. In times of the terrifying A and H symbols, those differences count. While in the initial stage the position of democracy might be less advantageous, in the long run a country based on a consensus of its citizens is strong and resilient, while states ruled by autocratic leaders, as experience teaches, break suddenly. They do not bend like iron in a fire—they break like steel.

Culture and Social-Psychological Factor; Leadership, Diplomacy

The socio-psychological factor is possibly the most difficult to analyze in precise terms, in terms on which a consensus of scholars could be easily reached. We know well that there is a common cultural pattern of a nation. This common cultural pattern was observed, described, since Herodotus. Tacitus gave a picture of the Germans which seems to be strangely real and enduring. Le Bon called it "national psychology," others "national character," "national culture." Evasive as this factor is, it still exists. No statesman can make decisions in foreign politics without evaluating a pattern of political behavior of a nation which is either his partner or his adversary. Nazi occupation of East Central Europe met with different forms of resistance. Resistance of the Poles was different from that of Czechs or Jugoslavs, especially Serbs. Of course many factors contributed to those differences, but national culture, dominant values, generally accepted patterns of political behavior formed an important factor. Foreign policy, whether for cooperation or conflict, sooner or later becomes a social process. Patterns of political behavior, or of general cultural patterns are thus paramount. Statesmen usually base their inferences on their own and historical experiences. Seldom if ever has a scientific framework been utilized. One may anticipate a pattern of behavior just on the basis of experience, without any scientific investigation, in a non-scientific way: Turks, when attacked by the Soviet army, may fight; similarly the Finns. Their history, cultural patterns form a basis for such inference. The German army, its discipline, ruthlessness, combined with efficiency, precision, are not false stereotypes, either. All such inferences are made on the level of a hypothesis—not findings.

Modern anthropology and sociology have made initial contributions to our understanding of national cultures and patterns of political behavior. We know today that culture, as well as attitudes, is not inborn, but culturally determined. Both are transmitted very early, from one generation to another, through the process of socialization. Through socialization a child is integrated into culture, into society. Primary groups—such as family, playgroups, play a paramount role in this process. Through this process mores and folkways as well as values and prejudices are transferred and perpetuated.

Man's motivation is deeply rooted in values. Values are both goals of our actions and yardsticks to measure our behavior. Values such as right and wrong, good and bad, honorable and dishonorable are guiding our behavior. There is an old and long discussion still going on as to whether values are common to all mankind; whether they are "absolute," having their own existence, "relative," different in every cultural setting; or whether there are any (not all) "universal" in character, common to all societies. Accordingly, three schools can be distinguished: absolute, relative, or universal. The latter argue that without certain values, such as cooperation, mutual aid, no society can exist; that those values can be empirically observed in every society, while other values, they admit, might be different.

For our purpose, it might be useful to accept a working proposition, which would recognize both cultural uniformity and variability, reflected in values.

A warning against overconfidence in our present methods of cultural analysis has to be added to our discussion. Easy explanation of cultures and values may be far removed from truth. Some cultural-anthropologists and psycho-analysts of wide repute attempted to explain Stalin's dictatorship by swaddling customs of Russian people. A swaddled child develops submissiveness to authority, and rebellion against it, some argued. The theory might be impressive, but hardly subject to any verification. Both facts—dictatorship and swaddling—might be well and accurately described. There is no causality, no "causal nexus" between those two facts.

Between the Scylla and Charybdis of cozy generalization, risky theories, there still is a stream of important knowledge and truth.

In foreign policy analysis ideology is both an objective and a factor. It is one of those overlapping concepts mentioned by the Brookings Institution's discussion of terms. "Cultural patterns" influence political ideologies. There is a difference between Italian nationalism, its extreme expression—Fascism —on one hand, and German extremist nationalism—Nazism— on the other hand. Differences between British, German, French, and Polish socialism can be partially explained by differences in national values, history, and social-economic conditions. Of course many values are common—hence uniformities in socialist ideology; some are different—responsible for variability. Personality structure of individuals, leaders, are influenced by those cultural differences.

Social-cultural analysis cannot be divorced from understanding of history, ideology, psychology. Historicism, as was mentioned already, was an important motivating force. In a nation there is not one ideology, but many ideologies. Each of them motivates a different social segment of the society. Understanding of those motivations and of the mechanism of mass movement is a part of analysis.

Foreign policy is not limited to formal relations between the governments. It is conducted on the level of governments and, in many instances, foreign policy objectives are carried over the borders by powerful social forces. The role of social forces in foreign policy, unfortunately, was better understood by totalitarians than by the professional, routinized diplomacy of Western democracies.

Since the time of the French revolution, social movements were an important force in foreign policy. The Communist parties all over the world as well as fellow travelers are an instrument of Soviet policy. So were German nationalistic organizations abroad an instrument of Nazi foreign policy. Democracies in their struggle for survival have to support and strengthen democratic forces over the world; in other words, social movements. This must not be done on the governmental level necessarily. It might be done by private organizations, similar in scope and ideas. This proposition may sound unorthodox, incompatible with rules of diplomacy. We are living, however, in very unorthodox times. A good diplomat should not waste much time at fashionable cocktail parties. A modern diplomat should know labor leaders, peasant leaders, union men—leaders of steel workers, miners; intellectuals, scholars. Here is a social milieu which reflects the nation.

Public opinion, morale, mass emotions belong also to this factor. Public opinion in foreign policy has been an area of detailed studies.[37]

"Morale" of a nation is difficult to reduce to precise scientific categories, similar to a well defined phenomenon of mass emotions. In spite of that, both are real and relevant. A statesman may speak about high "morale" of the Finns, dur-

[37] To mention only a few: Quincy Wright, ed., *Public Opinion and World Politics*, University of Chicago Press, 1933, Gabriel A. Almond's penetrating study *The American People and Foreign Policy*, Harcourt Brace, 1950; the well-written and readable Thomas A. Bailey's *The Man in the Street—The Impact of American Public Opinion on Foreign Policy*, Macmillan, 1948. In a number of countries, public opinion on foreign affairs is continuously explored. The *Public Opinion Quarterly* published at Princeton University is an important source of information. Public opinion polls have become very popular in the United States, and associated with the names of George Gallup and Elmo Roper. In September, 1953, a test was conducted to explore American public opinion towards problems of foreign policy, especially towards problems of cooperation. The results of this inquiry were published in *The Public Opinion Quarterly*, Vol. XVII, Winter 1953–54: "American Attitudes on World Organization," by Elmo Roper with an introduction by Thomas K. Finletter and comments by Frank W. Abrams, Norman Cousins, Paul G. Hoffman, Robert M. Hutchins, Mrs. Oswald B. Lord, Reinhold Niebuhr and Owen J. Roberts.

ing the first Finnish war. We know that this means constancy
of purpose, will to resist, will to carry on, in spite of sacrifices.
Such was the morale of a large segment of Poles and of the
British in their resistance during the battle of Britain.

Overt expressions of mass emotions, such as were released
by the Nazis, are an important element, too. A general
release of aggression through hate is a powerful political
engine. The Nazis, through release of feelings of hostility,
were able to build up emotional tensions, a kind of mass
hysteria, or even mass-psychosis. In such an emotional excite-
ment masses were easily led to conflict.

The social-psychological factor is closely connected with
the political-social factor; division has been made for purposes of analysis.

Leadership and diplomacy are factors of their own. Personality of leaders, who control focus of power, influences foreign
policy. It is especially important in totalitarian countries,
where power of dictators is not restrained by democratic
bodies, and where they exercise decisive influence over the
conduct of foreign policy. Maybe, foreign offices of the future
may have specialists in personality studies. Early understanding of personalities of Nazi Germany might have contributed
to the conduct of foreign affairs of the democratic countries.
Early discovery of authoritarian tendencies in personalities
might save future disappointments and risks. Policy oriented
toward peace and cooperation can hardly succeed with authoritarian, egocentric leaders.[37a]

Last but not least we must consider trained and able diplomacy. Countries of East-Central Europe, such as Poland, cannot defend themselves alone. They are far too weak vis à vis
the crushing weight of their neighbors. Good diplomacy and
good foreign policy was and is more important for the Polish

[37a] Harold D. Laswell made a contribution in the marginal field of
psychology and politics, sociology of politics. See his *The Political Writings of Harold D. Laswell* (Psychopathology and Politics; Politics: Who
Gets What, When, How; Democratic Character), 1951, Glencoe, Illinois,
The Free Press.

people, for their own survival than an army, for they can never create an army which would be in a position successfully to protect their citizens. Good diplomacy, and above all else wise foreign policy, may produce solutions on a regional, continental, and global level which will increase security, through cooperation and peace, that will create strength.

Factor X

Factors of foreign policy are not similar to those precise, well-cut stones which can be handled like single bricks in construction of a scholarly edifice. Dynamic, changing, overlapping, they are rather working propositions, than precise concepts which have to be adapted, cut, to a concrete, real situation. On a high level of abstractions a number of obvious factors can be singled out—but without a concrete situation, their weight, significance, cannot be evaluated. In various cases, in problem situations, significance of various factors may vary. Once factor A might be more relevant, another time factor B. Without a "context situation"—without a concrete situation—it is hardly possible to establish mutual relationship and significance of factors, as well as single out all of them. After all, division, distinction of factors is to an extent arbitrary, "artificial." The "problem situation" is a "natural phenomenon"—result of actions of men, of social forces. There are of course factors which were not mentioned in our discussion, and new factors may emerge in new, unexpected situations. Our division was based solely on past experience.

Is there, in other words, a factor X—to mention only chance, accident, irrational elements in human motivations, especially in politics? Even a physicist may expect in his experiment "the unexpected." Even his experiments are subject to accidents. In politics, chance, accidents play a significant role. Of course there are causes, variables which mature, germinate long, and can be observed early. But there are also accidents which affect the course of our actions; there is the element of chance.

Indeed, as Kirk rightly indicated, foreign policy analysis embraces the whole area of social sciences. So does the analysis of factors.

Those who make the foreign policy decisions, in choosing their strategic objectives, have to consider whether they possess adequate factors to support and enforce such objectives, whether the factors are adequate to form the material and spiritual instrumentality of a policy. Therefore, in reality, objectives, as well as policies, are related and depend upon factors. Either the objectives have to be adjusted to factors, or vice versa. The factors have to be adjusted and built up to be strong enough to support the objectives and policies. It might happen, however, that the existing factors are adequate to support the chosen objectives and policies, and an adjustment is not imperative. It requires wisdom and statesmanship to make proper estimates, proper analysis, for a decision concerning relationship between objectives, policies, and factors.

CHAPTER VI

Policies

Strategy and Tactics

ONCE plans have been outlined, a future vision unfolded, decisions made, then actions are devised to achieve the distant goals. Political ideology determines the strategy, directions of our policies, actions, toward distant, long-range, or strategic goals. If the ideology changes then, of course, strategy and strategic goals will change.

Long-range policy, or strategy, is broken down into short-range policies, or tactics. Tactical goals (short-range objectives) are stations in an advance toward strategic goals (long-range objectives). Short-range objectives may change continuously, as the situation, conditions, change, while long-range objectives may remain unchanged. Change in strategic goal is the grand change in policy.

For purposes of a working hypothesis only on an operational level, strategic goals can be viewed as causes; tactical goals and short-range policies as effects of long-range objectives. Selection of short-range (tactical) objectives and change of factors is often caused by the long-range (strategic) objectives or by changes in social, economic and political situation. The objectives of the Sudeten German nationalists, led by Henlein, in the Czechoslovakian parliament, were tactical objectives, subordinated to Hitler's long-range, strategic objectives—conquest of Czechoslovakia, Eastern Europe, Europe, Russia, the Planet.

A graphic scheme may give us a better picture of this interrelationship of various concepts. F stands for factors; F_1, F_2, F_3, F_4 indicates a number of various, mutually interrelated factors: F_1 for geographic; F_2, economic; F_3, demographic, et cetera. P stands for policies, T for tactical objectives, S for strategic objectives. T_1, T_2, T_3, similarly to Tx_1, Tx_2, Tx_3, stands for a variety of tactical objectives. P_1, P_2, P_3, as well as Px_1, Px_2, Px_3, Px_4, stand for a variety of short-range policies; all are a part of a long-range policy (LRP). Various policies (as in our scheme) are usually complementary, though on the surface they may give an impression of contradiction. Hitler's strategic aim—in the first stage—was conquest of Eastern

TABLE X

Structure of Foreign Policies

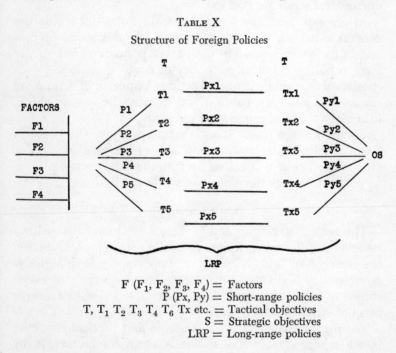

$$F\ (F_1, F_2, F_3, F_4) = \text{Factors}$$
$$P\ (Px, Py) = \text{Short-range policies}$$
$$T,\ T_1\ T_2\ T_3\ T_4\ T_6\ Tx\ \text{etc.} = \text{Tactical objectives}$$
$$S = \text{Strategic objectives}$$
$$LRP = \text{Long-range policies}$$

Europe as an initial stage toward more ambitious plans. Hitler's government signed a Polish-German friendship agreement, made friendly advances in the Balkans, campaigned against Austria and, further, supported a Nazi irredenta in Czechoslovakia, the U. S. A., Latin America, and all over Europe. Finally the Germans moved into Czechoslovakia. All those actions, policies, were not accidental—but complementary. They were the P_1, P_2, P_3 or Px_1, Px_2, Px_3, et cetera, of our chart. Every one of them was aimed at a tactical goal, T_1, T_2, or Tx_1, Tx_2 . . . , such as Polish-German peace treaty, disruption of Czechoslovakia—all together being a part of a long-range policy (LRP) toward a strategic objective S—world domination. Various policies and tactical objectives were complementary. Communist hostilities in Korea and Indochina, the cold war in Europe, the blockade of Berlin— all are policies (P) with tactical objectives (T) directed toward one central strategic goal (S).

In consequence, any policy has to be analyzed within the context situation, as a part of a more complex social process and in its interrelationship with other policies. A large scale foreign policy, especially a policy of conflict, seldom if ever consists of one, single course of action. A number of actions are released to paralyze, confuse and destroy the victim-nation, to achieve the long-range strategic goals.

Today, foreign policy is a global proposition, and requires a world outlook. An analyst must answer the question of how an observed course of action fits into the total, whole plan of a government, into the picture of world politics.

Stalin's Strategy

The terms "strategic" and "tactical" goal may have also a somewhat different meaning. In Stalin's strategy and tactics, the concept of "stages" plays an important role. The long-range policy is divided into stages—and objectives of every stage are called strategic. Tactics is concerned with achievement of strategic-stage goals.

We may translate Stalin's strategic and tactical concepts into a scheme (table XI). F stands again for factors, P for policies, T for tactical objectives, St-S for strategic-stage objectives. Factors are dynamic and approach to factors is based on Stalinist interpretation of historical materialism. In such an approach—agreements in Yalta, aggression in Korea, Indochina, occupation of Tibet, communization of China, are stages of a grand plan. Every one of those instances is what we may call a "strategic-stage objective." Concepts of

TABLE XI

Stalin's Strategy and Tactics

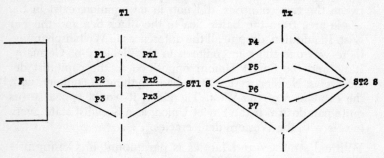

F = Factors
P(P$_1$, P$_2$, P$_3$ . . . Px$_1$, Px$_2$, etc.) = Policies
ST, Š, St$_2$S = Strategic-stage objectives

stages in foreign policy strategy are visualized in a proposal[38] of German-Soviet cooperation in 1939:

1. Referring to remarks by Astakhov about close collaboration and community of interests in foreign policy which formerly existed between Germany and Russia, I explained that such collaboration appeared attainable to me now, if the Soviet Government considered it desirable. I could visualize three stages:

Stage One: The reestablishment of collaboration in economic affairs through the credit and commercial treaty which is to be concluded.

Stage Two: The normalization and improvement of political relations. This included, among other things, respect for the interests of the other party in the press and in public opinion, and respect for the scientific and cultural activities of the other country. The official participation by Astakhov in German Art Day at Munich, or the invitation of German delegates to the Agricultural Exhibition in Moscow, as suggested by him to the State Secretary, could, for instance, be included under this heading.

Stage Three would be the reestablishment of good political relations, either a return to what had been in existence before (Berlin Treaty) or a new arrangement which took account of

[38] Nazi-Soviet Relations 1939–1941, Department of State, 1948, p. 32.

the vital political interests of both parties. This stage three appeared to me within reach, because controversial problems of foreign policy, which would exclude such a relationship between the two countries, did not, in my opinion, exist in the whole area from the Baltic Sea to the Black Sea and the Far East. In addition, despite all the differences in Weltanschauung, there was one thing in common in the ideology of Germany, Italy, and the Soviet Union: opposition to the capitalist democracies. Neither we nor Italy had anything in common with the capitalism of the West. Therefore, it would appear to us quite paradoxical if the Soviet Union, as a Socialist state, were to side with the Western democracies. . . .

Political strategy and tactics is paramount in Communist ideology. Lenin in *Proletarian Revolution and Renegade Kautsky* wrote: "Bolshevism can serve as model of tactics for all." Stalin in his articles on "Strategy and Tactics of the Russian Communists" (*Pravda*, 1923, No. 56) defined tactics as a part of strategy and subordinated to it. Stalin's article reads like excerpts from Clausewitz (he does not mention Clausewitz's name). He describes tactics as actions which are not concerned with war—or political struggle in general—, but with single battles, episodes, engagements. Later (in "Leninism," Vol. 1) Stalin develops the concept of stages in revolutionary struggle, and analyzes the revolution in those terms. "Strategy," he writes, "changes with the transition of revolution from stage to stage." However, strategy remains unchanged, the same, during the whole stage.[39]

Problems of strategy and tactics became relevant in politics of our century. Not all actions were planned *a priori* in terms of strategy and tactics. Sometimes courses of action were carefully prepared in those terms. In other cases, policy was just a "muddling through" expedient, from day to day, without an elaborated strategy. Once we look back, usually from hindsight, actions develop into a pattern, corresponding to strategy and tactics. Large-scale, elaborated foreign policies, like Hugh Gibson's foreign policy, are sooner or later framed

[39] Readings in Communist theory of strategy and tactics were published in a volume *Strategy and Tactics of the Proletarian Revolution*, Int. Publishers, New York, 1936.

into the pattern of strategy and tactics. The terminology may be different, but once we have foreign policy objectives —long and short range—then we have strategic and tactical objectives. Once actions are initiated, we have policies. So we have strategy and tactics.

Excerpts from a previous study of strategy and tactics will serve our discussion and purpose.[40]

Strategy and Tactics
(From "European Ideologies")[41]

A political program is often a minimum, actual proposition— a practical outline of demands for change, for immediate action, or for the maintenance of a status quo. A political program determines political tactics; the sum total of an ideology determines the great political strategy.

Clausewitz[42] defines tactics as the use of armed forces in engagement, and strategy as the use of engagements to attain the object of the war. Hence, political tactics denote the use of political forces in a current, actual, historical, concrete situation for cooperation with, or struggle against, other political forces; political strategy is the use of tactical moves to approach the great ideological objectives, determined by the whole ideology.

Political strategy and tactics correspond to "policy-making" and practical politics. Programs and tactics change more frequently than ideology and great political strategy. The former are constantly being adjusted to the ever-changing social and political situation; tactics, especially, must be speedily revised and arranged to fit the current change and distribution of political power. Political ideology, on the other hand, evolves more slowly; it constitutes the constant element, unlike the program, which constitutes the changing and adjustable portion of the policy. Political strategy, similarly, is relatively constant because of its long-range aims, while tactics are altered continuously. Strategical moves, even in an aggressive policy, may

[40] Strategy and tactics in political movements is also discussed by Rudolf Heberle, *Social Movements, An Introduction to Political Sociology*, Appleton, Century, Crofts, Inc., New York, 1951, pp. 359–408.

[41] Feliks Gross, ed., *European Ideologies*, Philosophical Library, New York, 1948, Chapter I, "Mechanics of European Politics," pp. 11–15.

[42] Karl von Clausewitz, *On War*, Chapter I, "Branches of the Art of War," p. 62, Modern Library Ed.

employ tactical retreats which do not necessarily denote a change in ideology or strategy. In political, as in military strategy, a tactical retreat is sometimes an essential part of the strategy of attack.

Inexperienced people often regard tactical moves as ideological changes. However, it is often very difficult to distinguish a tactical or strategical change from an ideological one.

When the United States and Canadian Communist Parties proclaimed their support of the free enterprise system, during World War II, it was actually only a tactical change. After the Allies took the lead and the enemy was finally defeated, Earl Browder was expelled from the Communist Party and its tactics changed again. But its ideology remained wholly unchanged, despite the dozens of books written by naive observers who happily asserted that it had been transformed.

The Communist Party in the United States expelled Mr. Browder with a barrage of publicity; the actual signal for this step was given in Paris by Duclos, the French Communist leader. This fact alone constitutes evidence that the Comintern's discipline and huge network remained intact, even though, for tactical reasons, the Comintern itself was declared dissolved.

In all totalitarian movements, the distinction between strategy and tactics plays a vital role. The correct analysis of any policy change (ideological and essential, or merely a tactical move), is of primary importance to the victims of the attack. Totalitarian movements usually employ Machiavellian political methods of treachery, false propaganda, and deceit. Their leaders often display exceptional ability in utilizing the four essential elements: ideology and program—strategy and tactics. When they revise their programs and tactics, publicizing this as a change in ideology, they usually find a highly receptive audience, since their victims, desiring peace, fall into wishful thinking. Machiavelli wrote, over four centuries ago: "Alexander VI did nothing else but deceive men, he thought of nothing else, and found occasion for it; no man was ever more able to give assurances, or affirmed things with stronger oaths, and no man observed them less; however, he always succeeded in his deceptions, as he well knew this aspect of things."[43]

[43] *The Prince,* Chapter XVIII, "In What Way Princes Must Keep Faith," p. 65, Modern Library Ed.

Modern totalitarian tacticians utilize this identical Machiavellian device and are often successful for a long period of time, before final defeat overtakes them. They deceive with oaths and promise that, due to a complete change of heart and mind, they have abandoned their objectives and revised their ideology. Shortly after, what the naive hailed and the propagandists publicized as a permanent, ideological change, proves to be merely a transient tactical retreat in preparation for a stronger attack.

It should be noted that programs and tactics may change, too, as a consequence of ideological development, such changes are of a more durable character and may represent a decisive change in the entire policy. In democratic parties the true nature of such changes is not a matter for secrecy and deceit.

When either a political party or a nation is forced to adjust her policy to an attack by a totalitarian movement, the analysis of tactics and program, of ideology or strategy is of foremost importance. Only a change in ideology indicates a lasting change in policy; programmatic and tactical changes mainly denote a struggle for a more strategic position for the final attack.

As previously mentioned, ideology is the most constant element; after it comes strategy which influences program and tactics. Tactics is the most variable element.

Totalitarian governments often use tactics to cover up strategic goals, to confuse the opponent. Democratic governments are restrained in deceit and double-talk. Firstly, this is contrary to democratic principles, and, secondly, the process of policy decisions is in large measure open to public information. In a democracy strategic goals are stated and discussed in public, parliamentary debates.

A conversation of a German Foreign Office representative, Schnurre, with Soviet Chargé in Berlin, Astakhov, reflects the use of tactics as "camouflage." The conversation quoted here is an excerpt from Schnurre's secret memorandum of July 27, 1939.[43a]

In my reply I pointed out that German policy in the East had taken an entirely different course in the meantime. On our part

---

[43a] *Nazi-Soviet Relations, 1939–1941*, Documents from the Archives of the German Foreign Office, Edited by Raymond J. Sontag and James S. Beddie, Department of State, Washington, D.C., 1948, p. 34.

there could be no question of menacing the Soviet Union; our aims were in an entirely different direction. Molotov, himself, in his last speech had called the Anti-Comintern Pact camouflage for an alliance aimed against the Western democracies.

The "Problem Paper" Approach

In a policy analysis we act as observers; in a policy formulation, we assume a position of policy makers.

A method of policy formulation was devised by the research staff of the Brookings Institution, under the direction of the late Dr. Leo Pasvolsky. The method was called "problem paper" approach, though it seems to me that "alternative" approach might be a more appropriate term.

The process of policy formulation is, of course, different in different countries and different foreign offices. There are not any uniform rules. The Brookings Institution staff, especially Dr. Leo Pasvolsky, however, developed a method which follows the principles of scientific research and permits a wide exploration of the problem. As an educational device it is a highly challenging and fruitful approach.

The process starts with a problem paper. In international relations, we have a number of "problems" connected with a definite situation. Formulation of a policy is geared to a problem and to objectives. During the Second World War Soviet troops entered Polish territory and the Soviet authorities created their own Lublin government. For American and British policy-makers, who still recognized the London government in exile, this was a problem-situation. A problem may arise when principles, commitments, objectives, or actions of a government—for instance, the United States government—meet with attitudes, behavior, or actions of other governments. This was the case with Soviet policies during and after the Second World War, as in the Polish case. In other situations strategic objectives may favor tactical objectives, or settlements which contradict principles. American policy of containment of Communist advance, may favor support for colonial policies of its allies, which contradict the principle of self-determination of nations. American policy toward Franco Spain, establishment of bases, is a tactical move (or "stage-strategic goal") in a policy of containment, defense against further advance of communism. This policy is inconsistent with principles of democracy, with the concept of "Free World," and antagonizes some of America's allies. It is a problem.[44]

Actions of a government, state, which involve security of the United States and its allies—or endanger peace of the world—is a typical and serious situation, which may be defined as "problem" in international relations. Similarly actions oriented toward peace, cooperation, which require actions, cooperation of another state, create a "problem." Plans for a European federation met with reluctance of the British government, which was and is reluctant to join a continental federal system. Part of French public opinion, prominent statesmen, hesitate to enter a close union with Germany without the British, without an adequate counter-balance of the German influence in such a union. The United States government supports integration of Western Europe, which in turn is a part of the Atlantic Community. Difficulties in European cooperation create an international problem for United States foreign policy.

The problem paper consists of statement of the problem, description of situation, and proposed policies called "alternatives." Here are a few problems, formulated by the staff of the Brookings Institution:

> The problem is to determine the means by which the United States can best develop its position among the free nations in order to reduce the threat of Soviet power to international peace and security.[45]

On problems of regionally organized economic activities:

> The problem is to determine what steps the United States should take to minimize the conflict between the regional or-

[44] For fuller discussions of the concept "problem" see: *Major Problems of United States Foreign Policy, 1952–53*, The Brookings Institution, Washington, D.C., 1953, pp. 101 ff.

[45] op. cit. p. 108.

ganization of economic activity and the effort to maintain a world-wide system of trade and payment.[46]

On problems of recovery and rearmament in Western Europe:

The problem is to determine what additional steps the United States should take to help Western Europe bear the burden of rearmament.[47]

On problem of underdeveloped areas:

The problem is to reconsider the Point IV Program in order to decide what the objectives of the United States should be in offering this kind of aid and to determine whether the present program is well adapted to achieve those objectives.[48]

The problem is stated, as it confronts the United States, and a general, social, political, economic background of the problem is given. In consequence, the first part of the problem paper is mostly a scholarly and detached description of the situation, based on facts, carefully selected and checked. To use our terminology—it is a description on a higher level of verification—level of findings. It is not any more a general hypothesis, a hypothesis based on a limited and rather haphazard collection of facts.

Preparation of a problem paper may also be an educational exercise. Such a paper might be assigned to a group of students. They start with the problem-statement; from there they proceed with their research. Of course, their universe of facts is limited to sources available for the public. The situation, background, factors are described in a dispassionate way, objectively, as far as man's values permit. Those facts and inferences of the descriptive part serve then as a basis of policy formulation.

Alternatives

A problem is stated, the analyst now proceeds with a question: "What can I do?" and answers this question, suggesting a policy. Once a policy is suggested, the next question

[46] op. cit. p. 127.
[47] op. cit. p. 136.
[48] op. cit., p. 144.

follows: "What else can I do?" and usually the answer is, "a number of things can be done." A number of policies—not solely one—are usually possible and feasible. They are called "alternatives"—with a blessing from H. W. Fowler of the *Modern English Usage*. The term "alternative" is used here not as a pair of possibilities from which only one can be selected, but as a set of possibilities from which any one can be chosen. The analyst is trying to find as many alternatives as he can, those he likes as much as the others of which he personally disapproves. In consequence, an analyst suggests from the large number of alternatives a "preferred" policy he regards as most appropriate.

The merit of this method is that it permits exploration of a number of possibilities—it opens a wide arc of various possible solutions open to an intelligent choice. Instead of passion and emotion, a path is wide open for exercise of intelligence and restraint, for dispassionate evaluation of a possible course of action.

Several alternatives may be complementary, others contradictory, conflicting. In the latter case choice of one policy may conflict with other choices. "The value of the analytical method illustrated here is that it emphasizes the importance of not making a final choice until the entire range of alternatives and of their relationships have been subjected to a rigorous examination," explain the authors of *The Major Problems of United States Foreign Policy 1952–53*, in an introductory note on alternative approach.[49]

According to the late Dr. Leo Pasvolsky the method originated out of an episode during President Roosevelt's administration. An expert had been invited by the President to analyze a situation and suggest a policy. President Roosevelt was not satisfied, however, with his suggestion and asked "What else can I do?" He postponed his decision and asked for other alternatives. The advancement of this method, its broad application in the field of education, was a contribution of Dr. Pasvolsky and of the Institution's competent and gifted staff.

[49] op. cit., p. 313.

Brookings Institution and Development of the Alternative Approach

Since 1947 seminars have been organized by the Brookings Institution. The meetings were held in Stanford, Duke, Harvard, Lake Forest, Princeton, Pittsburgh, Washington (St. Louis), Dartmouth, Virginia and other universities. The conference at Farmington (Virginia University) was entirely devoted to teaching methods (in international relations). Statesmen, diplomats, government experts from various government departments, including the Army, Navy, and Air Force, representatives of business, labor, university and college professors, were invited to those seminars. The Brookings Institution staff prepared problem papers. They were distributed for study to all the members of the seminars, and carefully studied. Indeed, experienced statesmen, ambassadors, and university professors were studying them with interest and attention in student dormitories. Many had an impression that they had returned to school. After papers were studied, the seminars were broken into a number of "round tables." At every "round table" a different problem paper was discussed. Each set of round tables was followed by a general session where main points were digested, and results of the work of round tables discussed. Meetings were held as a rule on university campuses, which were somewhat remote from the noise and pressure of the city. Members of the Brookings seminar were living a campus life again; they ate together, met frequently. Some of the seminars, as the Lake Forest seminar, lasted almost two weeks. During this whole period the interest, reading, discussion, of the invited guests were focussed around international affairs, foreign policy, its specific problems, and method. It was an "adult education" of a group of highly educated men and women, many of whom wrote books, edited newspapers and journals, made policy decisions, commanded navies, and had the modesty and enthusiasm to learn again. Discussions were carefully recorded, and the problem papers were later revised in light of those discussions and published in book form as *Major Problems of United States Foreign Policy.*

The method went through the fire of many discussions; it survived well the penetrating criticism, and was applied to many, diverse and different international problems.

The problem method approach and techniques of Brookings seminars, their organization, is well illustrated in one of the early memoranda of the Lake Forest Seminar of June 4, 1949.

Lake Forest Seminar's Memorandum

The problem under consideration is identified and described from the viewpoint of the general and specific objectives that the United States seeks to attain with regard to it. It is then analyzed with reference to its origin, its importance to the United States, and its development. This is followed by a statement of the main issues to which the problem gives rise; of several alternative courses of action open to the United States for the resolution of each issue; and of the principal implications of, and arguments for and against, each particular course of action. All this is done in the light of the general guiding principles and objectives of United States foreign policy; the state of public opinion; the attitudes of other governments; the relation of the particular problem to other problems confronting the United States; and the numerous other factors at home and abroad that condition the conduct of foreign relations.

Up to this point, the problem papers follow general governmental practice, except that papers prepared in the government reflect the use of confidential and oftentimes highly secret information available to the public. Another important difference is that our papers stop with the analysis of the issues and alternative courses of action, whereas official papers are carried a step further, which is to recommend to policy-deciding officials a preferred course of action. Since our purpose is to demonstrate a technique of analysis and discussion rather than to reach conclusions, this final step is omitted from our problem papers. The latter are intended to provide the basis for each participant to reach his own conclusion and, perhaps more important, to keep in mind the courses of action rejected and the reasons for so doing.

While our problem papers illustrate a general type of analysis that is applicable to the entire process of policy-making, they are intended to demonstrate only some of the many phases involved in that process. Policy-making takes place in several stages and at several levels. It deals with a continuous stream of problems, which arise because the United States or other countries want to pursue a certain course of action. The problems may be short-range or long-range in character. They may call for immediate or proximate action. They may be problems of anticipation.

Whenever the government must come to a decision on a problem, the officials concerned must first determine whether possible action falls within the framework of a previously established policy or whether it requires the formulation of a new policy. The formulation, if necessary, of a new policy constitutes the next stage of the policy-making process. In either case, there is then a need to determine the best means of giving effect to the policy that is to govern the situation, bearing in mind that a course of action may directly influence the content, nature and direction of the policy. Finally, occasions frequently arise for a periodic or ad hoc review of the established policy or of measures taken to give effect to it, in the light of further study, or difficulties of implementation, or changed circumstances, or any other pertinent factors. In practice, these stages frequently overlap, but they are, nevertheless, clearly distinguishable, and they all require basically the type of analysis described above.

It should be noted that these steps in the policy-making process—even when major decisions are involved—may take place with little or nothing committed to writing and merely by way of oral discussion. Moreover, decisions are at times made hastily, without reference to other policies or with insufficient coordination among the policy-makers. But when the more formal process, based on the preparation and discussion of problem papers, is used—as it frequently is for both major and minor decisions—it usually begins at a level at which all pertinent materials are assembled and analyzed and the main issues and alternative courses of action are identified and discussed—all this preparatory to recommending a preferred course of action. The actual recommendations may be formulated at the same level and reviewed at higher levels, or they may be formulated entirely at the higher levels. Eventually, they find their way to the highest officials—in some cases, the President himself—for final decision.

Our problem papers are intended to illustrate this process mainly in the stage of planning for the implementation of an established policy and at the level at which the laborious task of assembling and analyzing materials necessary for policy-making is performed. The reason is that these phases of the process are least familiar to those outside the government.

In arranging for the discussion of the problem papers at the Seminar, we ask the participants to put themselves in the position of government officials charged with the duty of exploring possible courses of action for giving effect to an already deter-mined policy. These officials may or may not agree with the pol-icy, but their immediate task is to find ways of applying it, rather than to review it. In the same way, the discussion of the prob-lem papers in the round-table sessions at the Seminar is intended to proceed within the framework of the existing official policy on the problem under consideration, with primary emphasis on the various ways open to the government of the United States of implementing that policy. This does not imply that either the authors of the paper or the participants in the Seminar necessarily approve the official policy.

In previous Seminars, there was a general and understandable tendency to begin round-table discussions by questioning the official policy. That is, of course, a proper and important pro-cedure, but it belongs to other phases of policy-making rather than those demonstrated through the problem papers. In order to provide an opportunity for this type of discussion, we have arranged to devote a plenary session, following each set of round-table sessions, to a consideration of the wisdom of the existing official policy on the problem in question and of pos-sible alternative policies that might be adopted.

There is one important difference in the form of the four problem papers. Whereas in Problem Papers I, II and III, the analysis of issues relates to a number of alternative courses of action with accompanying arguments, in Problem Paper IV only one course of action is indicated under each issue, the one that has been officially proposed. The task of devising other al-ternative courses of action is left in this case to the participants in the Seminar. This affords a variation in the technique of dis-cussion that previous experience has suggested as desirable.

Details of the Seminar Program

Opening Plenary Session

The opening plenary session will be devoted to an explanation of the purposes of the Seminar, of the procedures to be followed, and of any administrative arrangements that need to be brought to the attention of the participants.

Discussion of Problem Papers

In the case of each problem paper, there will be, first, a brief introductory plenary session designed to bring the material contained in the paper up to date. Immediately, thereafter, the participants will divide into four round-table groups, each of which will follow the same agenda, consisting of two parts, as follows:

Part 1: a consideration of the first two sections of the problem paper ("Statement of the Problem" and "Development of the Problem"), with a view to a clarification of:

(a) The nature and origin of the problem;
(b) The nature of, and reasons for, the existing official policy with regard to it;
(c) The precise objectives sought by the United States through the application of that policy; and
(d) The relation of the problem and of the policy to other problems confronting the United States and to other policies pursued by the United States.

Part 2: a consideration of the issues set forth and discussed in the concluding section of the problem paper ("Main Issues and Alternatives of Action"), on the basis of the following questions for each issue:

(a) How significant is the issue as stated for the attainment of the objectives sought by the United States with regard to the problem in question?
(b) Do the alternative courses of action listed under that issue constitute the most feasible possibilities from which a choice should be made in arriving at a decision? If not, what other possibilities should be listed?
(c) Are the main implications of the various alternative courses of action, and the principal arguments for and

against each, adequately brought out in the problem paper? If not, what other considerations should be taken into account?

(d) *If time permits,* which of the alternative courses of action suggested under (b) and (c) above should be regarded as the preferred one?

The round tables may wish to discuss the selection of issues made in the problem paper.

There will be a plenary session following each set of round-table sessions. This will provide an opportunity for a brief presentation of the main points brought out in the round-table discussions, but the major portion of the session will be devoted to a review of the existing official policy on the problem under consideration.

The agenda described above will apply in full to the discussions of Problem Papers I, II and III. A slight variation will be introduced in the discussion of Problem Paper IV because of the differences in the presentation of the issues and the alternative courses of action in the paper itself.

Final Plenary Sessions

At the two plenary sessions on Friday, July 1, the broad world picture and the role of the United States in world affairs will be discussed, mainly on the basis of a memorandum to be distributed at Lake Forest. The participants in the Seminar may also find it useful to re-read in this connection Part I of the Brookings Institution's volume on *Major Problems of United States Foreign Policy, 1948–49,* especially pages 9–26. An attempt will be made to relate to this broader material the subject matter of the four problems. Copies of the volume will be available at the Seminar. . . .

A problem paper on underdeveloped areas (*Major Problems of United States Foreign Policy, 1952–53,* Brookings Institution, pp. 347–351) may serve as a good illustration of the method.

Alternative Approach to
Underdeveloped Areas

What action should the United States take when contradictions arise between its policies for the acquisition of raw mate-

*rials and its policies and programs for the economic advance-
ment of the producing areas?*

In many of the countries that supply raw materials, purchases
by the United States and actions to develop new sources of supply impinge directly and indirectly on the plans of these countries for long-range economic development. The extent to which
these actions are consistent with over-all development plans is
of major interest to the United States. It has adopted as a matter
of policy the position that aiding underdeveloped countries on
a long-term basis is a prerequisite to creating the economic
well-being on which lasting world peace depends.

The issue to be considered is the difficult one of weighing the
short-run importance of obtaining the materials immediately
needed against the long-run importance of assuring that projects
in the producing countries will contribute to the lasting development of these areas and therefore to the ultimate strength of
the non-Communist world. This dilemma is illustrated by the
fact that the urgency of the problem of materials often tends to
submerge or run counter to sound development plans, despite
the fact that both accomplishments are equally important to
the security of the United States. In this dilemma there appear
to be three principal courses of action to choose from:

Alternative One is to give priority to the procurement of raw
materials.

Alternative Two is to give priority to raw materials, but to
take long-run economic development into account by compensating for the adverse effects of raw materials policies or taking maximum advantage of whatever contribution these policies
can make toward sound economic development.

Alternative Three is to give priority to the objective of securing well-balanced economic development and adjust policies
on raw materials accordingly.

Alternative One—to give priority to the procurement of raw
materials—assumes that the problem of getting the materials
to support the rearmament effort and to meet immediate requirements is so acute that it must be solved regardless of the
consequences in terms of long-run objectives.

The main arguments that may be advanced *in favor of* this
alternative are as follows:

1. If the United States is unsuccessful in obtaining the materials it needs, it may not only be unable to prevent a general war but may lose such a war. In that case the United States would be impotent to carry out any long-range assistance programs.

2. Priority for raw materials will not necessarily interfere with desirable long-run development. Expenditures to expand the production of materials may automatically aid in promoting the economic well-being of the producing countries. These projects will provide employment and create foreign exchange earnings to improve the financial position of the exporting countries and will enable them to purchase needed equipment and machinery when it becomes available.

The main arguments that may be advanced *against* this alternative are as follows:

1. Defense against communism involves not simply the building of military strength in the industrial nations of the West, but the building of economic defenses against poverty and therefore against the threat of Communist subversion that such conditions invite. To place major emphasis on the one and neglect the other may create a fatal weakness in the defenses of the West.

2. Actions taken to develop additional sources of raw materials intensify those problems in the producing areas that result from an over-reliance on exports. The immediate desirability of obtaining materials must be weighed against the possibility of undermining the long-run economic position of the producing areas.

3. It would be unwise to assume that long-range development programs are politically unimportant during the defense period, when the United States is striving to promote a maximum degree of international co-operation.

Alternative Two—to give priority to raw materials, but to take long-run economic development into account by compensating for the adverse effects of raw materials policies or taking maximum advantage of whatever contribution these policies can make toward sound economic development—implies that while first importance attaches to getting the raw materials that are needed, this fact does not justify disregarding the effect of these activities on the long-term aspirations of the producing countries.

The main arguments that may be advanced *in favor of* this alternative are as follows:

1. Since only a relatively small amount of money is available to promote the development of the underdeveloped areas, advantage should be taken of the much larger sums being used to buy raw materials by channeling these wherever possible into avenues that will promote both short-run supply objectives and long-run economic development.

2. The dollar earnings of the producing countries that result from the stepped-up purchases of materials could make an important contribution to long-range objectives if appropriate steps are taken by the United States. These might include the granting of a higher priority for the delivery of needed capital equipment; guarantees of the purchasing power of current export earnings in terms of future delivery of manufactured goods; greater use of long-term purchase contracts to promote stability in the producing areas; aid in establishing processing plants in the producing countries; development of agricultural techniques to balance the shift of productive resources into mining and other export industries and assistance in managing fiscal problems arising from the raw materials bonanza.

3. It is highly desirable to make sure that projects to increase the supply of raw materials do not run counter to plans for the development of more balanced economies. To the extent that they do, the cost of assistance to correct the situation may be far greater than the cost of proceeding now to conform to a sound development program.

The main arguments that may be advanced *against* this alternative are as follows:

1. The development of relationships between projects for the procurement of materials and Point IV projects might give rise to propaganda charges of American imperialism by shifting the emphasis from helping less fortunate people to helping ourselves. Such action would damage the idealistic aspect of the Point IV Program and might render the whole concept of such assistance unacceptable to some countries.

2. In many cases it would not be possible for policies on materials to be geared into the economic development plans of the producing countries. Inconsistency between the methods of acquiring materials and long-range economic development plans

is illustrated by the fact that projects to increase the supply of materials often strengthen industrial interests in the supplying area, which may be the least sympathetic toward improving economic conditions for the mass of the population or otherwise promoting the objectives of the Point IV type of development.

3. If policies with respect to materials threaten to defeat the broader objective of building long-run economic strength and friendship in the underdeveloped areas, the desirable action would be to abandon such policies rather than attempt to compensate for them.

Alternative Three—to give priority to the objective of securing well-balanced economic development and adjust policies on raw materials accordingly—affirms the position that the needs of the moment for materials are not so overriding as to justify the abandonment of development programs. The consequences of this position might be to reduce the availability of materials for defense, or require further temporary cutbacks in civilian production.

The main arguments that may be advanced *in favor of* this alternative are as follows:

1. Improved conditions in the underdeveloped areas would do more to strengthen the free world and build resistance against communism than an unqualified concentration on improving the supply position of the consuming countries.

2. The problem is not simply to get more materials from the producing areas and then get out. The dependence of the consuming countries on many of these sources of materials will continue into the indefinite future. It is necessary to begin now to provide a sound basis for future development through technical assistance to train workers in more efficient methods, improvement in health to make more efficient work possible; and improvements in housing, food supply, and education. Comprehensive development programs to break the vicious circle of poverty and low productivity are basic requirements to assure not only Point IV objectives but to provide raw materials for the industrialized nations on a long-term mutually satisfactory basis.

3. From the standpoint of security the position of the United States would be improved by moving forward now with long-range development programs to achieve the improvements in

economic conditions that give meaning to membership in the community of free nations, leaving the acquisition of materials to be a secondary objective. This is the approach successfully followed by the Economic Cooperation Administration in the conduct of overseas development and strategic materials programs. Conflicts between the two programs were resolved as far as possible in favor of the economies of the producing countries.

The main arguments that may be advanced *against* this alternative are as follows:

1. In view of the heavily burdened American economy, expenditures in foreign countries should be limited to aid that can make a direct and immediate contribution to the defense effort. Public and congressional support for the Point IV Program cannot be expected to continue unless some immediate return in an increased supply of raw materials can be realized.

2. It is impossible to carry out long-range economic development plans now. Neither the funds nor the capital goods required for a broad program of development are available. It will be necessary to accept this as the immediate fact, and work the long-term development objectives into the program for the acquisition of materials rather than attempt the reverse.

3. Making the program for materials contingent on conforming to long-range development programs would be an administrative task of the greatest complexity. The urgency of the situation would not justify the acceptance of such difficulties.

Use of Alternatives as Mode of Thinking in Politics

Critics of the alternative approach argue that most of its application is purely academic. Usually, they argue, we decide upon a policy, before we explore the alternatives. The new alternatives contribute little, they say, as selection of a course of action is made on the basis of definite premises, which determine definite policies. The alternative approach however, is neither purely academic nor entirely new. It is a generally accepted mode of thought, applied in our culture frequently, also in politics and military planning. Those thought patterns can be observed as social facts. Evaluation of alternatives in politics was made in the East and in the

West, long before the Brookings Institution's staff began to
formulate, apply and polish the method. The contribution
of the latter is rather in a precise description of operation,
and in application of scientific principles to research. The
alternatives were applied before by policy makers who spend
little time on evaluating the method, and plenty of it on
policy decision. In 1939 representatives of Great Britain and
France negotiated with Soviet representatives in Moscow a
possible alliance to check the Nazi advance. The Soviet government negotiated simultaneously with the Nazi government in Berlin. Some Soviet and British diplomats analyzed
the situation in 1939, in the days of the mortal perils and
tensions, similarly. The Soviet government had more alternatives to choose from than one. Stalin chose a German-Soviet
agreement.

The British representative, Mr. Strang, wrote on June 21,
1939, from Moscow:

> It is we, not the Russians, who took the initiative in starting
> negotiations. Our need for an agreement is more immediate
> than theirs. . . . We have no other policy open to us than that
> of building up the Peace Front. The Russians have, in the last
> resort, at least two alternative policies—namely, the policy of
> isolation and the policy of accommodation with Germany. . . .
> If we want an agreement with them we shall have to pay their
> price or something very near to it.[50]

At the same time, on June 15, 1939, a German foreign office
representative reports the following conversation:

Foreign Office Memorandum

Berlin, June 15, 1939.

The Bulgarian minister called on me today and told me con-
fidentially the following: The Soviet Russian Chargé, with
whom he had no intimate relations, called on him yesterday
without any apparent reason and stayed with him two hours.

[50] *Documents on British Foreign Policy 1919–1939.* Edited by E. L. Wood-
ward and Rohan Butler assisted by Anne Orde. Third Series, Volume VI,
1939. London: Stationary Office, 1953, Doc. No. 376, p. 422.

The long conversation, of which it could not be ascertained whether it had reflected the personal opinions of Herr Astakhov or the opinions of the Soviet Government, could be summarized approximately as follows:

The Soviet Union faced the present world situation with hesitation. She was vacillating between three possibilities, namely the conclusion of the pact with England and France, a further dilatory treatment of the pact negotiations, and a rapprochement with Germany. This last possibility, with which ideological considerations would not have to become involved, was closest to the desires of the Soviet Union. In addition there were other points, for instance that the Soviet Union did not recognize the Rumanian possession of Bessarabia. The fear of a German attack, however, either via the Baltic countries or via Rumania was an obstacle. In this connection the Chargé had also referred to *Mein Kampf*. If Germany would declare that she would not attack the Soviet Union or that she would conclude a nonaggression pact with her, the Soviet Union would probably refrain from concluding a treaty with England. However, the Soviet Union did not know what Germany really wanted, aside from certain very vague allusions. Several circumstances also spoke for the second possibility, namely to continue to conduct the pact negotiations with England in a dilatory manner. In this case the Soviet Union would continue to have a free hand in any conflict which might break out.

. . . At the end Herr Draganoff repeated again that he had no indications why Herr Astakhov had given him this information. He was pondering the possibility that this was probably done with the intention of having Herr Draganoff report it to us.[51]

It is evident that the purpose of this conversation was transmission of its content to the Nazi authorities.

The British representative, Mr. Strang saw, in fact, not two but three alternative policies open to the Soviet government: 1) an alliance with Great Britain and France, 2) isolation, 3) accommodation with Nazi Germany.

The Soviet chargé, Astakhov, saw three possibilities too: 1)

[51] *Nazi-Soviet Relations, 1939–1941*, Documents from the Archives of the German Foreign Office, Edited by Raymond J. Sontag and James S. Beddie, Department of State, Washington, D.C., 1948, p. 20.

an alliance with Great Britain and France, 2) dilatory treatment of the pact of negotiations, 3) *rapprochement* with Germany.

Although British and Soviet objectives were different, and although Mr. Strang was a British diplomat of conservative or liberal views, and Astakhov a Communist, they saw the situation in a very similar way. Mr. Astakhov shelved his dialectics, used instead his common sense, and so he was able to arrive at a proper estimate of the situation. From those three choices Stalin chose the third one—and practically pulled the trigger which released the war. It was Stalin's "preferred policy," which lubricated the conflict process and prepared an attack against the Soviet Union. Hitler's attacking the Soviet Union prepared his doom. Neither Stalin's nor Hitler's choice from the point of view of their interest was an intelligent one.

In the great days of victory in 1944 and 1945 alternative approach to military and political strategy was applied too. Winston Churchill writes about the alternative operations discussed in Teheran—and their combinations. Every one of those operations had its symbol: *Overlord*—was the main operation, in north-western France; amphibious landing in the south of France was called *Anvil* (also called later *Dragoon*); the third operation suggested in 1944 by Churchill was the Balkan operation—this was rejected.[52] All alternatives were complementary. In foreign policy formulation, the Soviet Union's participation in war against Japan was an alternative problem. Two alternatives were open to the British and American governments in 1944 and 1945: the Soviet Union's participation in war against Japan or its isolation from this war, in view of possible implications. In the midst of the war, when the paramount objective is victory, and preservation of human life, Soviet participation was an "of course" preferred policy.

During the Bermuda conference (December 1953) alternatives were used as a mode of thinking. Problems of a Euro-

[52] Winston Churchill, *The Second World War*, Vol. VI, Book 1, The New York Times, October 26, 1953.

pean Army—it seems—have been entertained in those terms by the Big Three:[53]

> High American officials, in analyzing the results of the conference, emphasized that the United States has not yet abandoned hope of eventually achieving a European Army, although they acknowledged that for the first time the Big Three leaders had touched briefly on the alternatives to it, none of them attractive . . .

Alternatives were also considered in case an agreement on European Defense Community should fail. Hanson W. Baldwin[54] reported that other alternatives were considered, "that there were other things to be done," as Secretary Dulles has phrased it. The other alternatives were:

> 1. A do-nothing policy, or a policy of drift. Such a policy would avoid final decision between West Germany and France, would permit some flexibility in diplomacy and would hope that events, rather than men, might create circumstances that would make ratification possible in some indefinite future. . . .
> 2. A policy that would emphasize the political and economic aspects of European union and would postpone the military aspects. . . .
> 3. An invitation to West Germany to join the North Atlantic Treaty Organization and to rearm as part of it.

Here is another example of "alternative approach" in foreign policy in its practical application.

Presentation of the alternative method, similarly to strategy and tactics, may leave the impression that it works best in a conflict situation. Both concepts have, however, the same application in policy of cooperation. They are instrumentalities, tools, and can be applied for a variety of goals. Tools are neutral—goals of men are not, they contain the values. In policies of cooperation various "alternatives" were and are considered too. In a plan for world organization, such as the United Nations, a number of alternatives are possible, to

[53] New York Herald Tribune, December 8, 1953.
[54] Hanson W. Baldwin, "The French Crisis, II, Alternatives to European Army Plan Are Viewed Politically Defective," *New York Times*, December 25, 1953.

mention only the well-known issue of veto against another alternative—elimination of veto power in the Security Council. One alternative is a world organization based on regional systems—the other, a world organization without a regional system, based on direct participation of member-states. In the Council of Europe in Strasbourg, three alternatives of European integration were advanced: inter-governmental, functional, federalistic. The first suggested solely cooperation between governments without further integration; second—integration wherever real need and purpose is present; third—federal integration or merger of states. The Schuman Plan, European Defense Community, are examples of the successful functional alternative. Although the methods were not elaborate, and approach not necessarily detached and cool, still the fundamental concept of choice, of alternative solutions, was used.

Concepts of strategy and tactics can be similarly applied for peace. Our strategic goal in the Near East is security and peace. This requires understanding between Israel and the Arab states. The United States relief for Arab refugees combined with an Israeli effort might be not solely a limited, humanitarian goal—but could become a tactical move to achieve a strategic goal of international policy—peace and security in the Near East—and a broader humanitarian goal—brotherhood of men.

PART 3

CHAPTER VII

Forecast

To unravel this existent past in the present and on the basis of it to previse future is the task of science.

G. H. MEAD

"Scientism" and Forecast

'PREDICTION," "anticipation," "forecast" . . . all those terms still invite contempt among many social scientists. A true scholar studies "what is." "What will happen" is an area of prophesy, many academicians argue. Prediction might be a proper thing for quack doctors, but not for true Ph.D.'s. We understand the past far better than the future and we like and know how to apply the past for its understanding. Western thinking is largely historical. Past experiences, as they were recorded, as we lived through them, shape our views of the present and often shape our goals of the future.

Academic reluctance to deal with problems of the future is not the result of a narrow approach to society or science. It is rather a consequence of the very concept of science and empiricism. The scientific method requires facts, known facts, which can be described, classified and checked. Known facts are located in the past and present. In the future new facts will arise again, in this boundless process of change. They cannot, however, be described now, at present. They cannot be seen, they cannot be checked and verified now—only somewhere in the distant future—and verification is precisely an essential part of scientific method. Not all, but many social scientists had and still have, therefore, a critical approach to any prediction, anticipation. In natural sciences the situation

155

is different. Discovery of what is called natural laws, or better, universals, permit one to anticipate. We can predict that heat will cause expansion of iron. Our iron or steel bridges, are laid accordingly; space is permitted between various iron and stone parts for we predict that stone and metal will expand in summer. Multiple causation, however, makes prediction in social sciences much more complex, difficult, than in natural sciences. Still, one of the paramount functions of science is to give us this magic power of prediction and control as means for achieving a better society, and above all for a better world for the individual.

All difficulties in social sciences granted, forecasting is important in foreign policy. A foreign policy is released into the future—not in the past. A foreign policy decision must take into account a future situation. In consequence the field of foreign politics needs statesmen and experts trained in understanding of the future, trained in tracing the possible trend, possible situations.

Hugh Gibson argues that anticipation of future developments is one of the main functions of a foreign office. Without looking ahead, no foreign policy is possible—he argues, and he sees "a fundamental obstacle in having foreign policy" in the fact that ". . . the department has come not only to quiesce but even to refuse to look ahead. . . . Ironically enough, in the State Department and the Foreign Service we have the machinery for anticipating future developments. Fundamentally, according to any reasonable estimate, that is what the services are there for."[55] Foresight is not encouraged, Ambassador Gibson continues, but, rather, frowned upon. Of course anticipation does not mean the use of soothsayers. However, he believes that a man in the field, with a good understanding of a situation, has a picture of things to come. Since his book was written much has changed. Already in 1947, in the Office of the Undersecretary of State, a Policy Planning Staff was established for assuring the development of long-range policy. Its purpose is not solely advice on formulating and developing policies for achievement of American foreign policy objectives, but also *"anticipating problems* (my italics) which

[55] op. cit., p. 148-9.

the Department may encounter in discharge of its mission."
Anticipating is forecasting: here the function of a state department in foreign policy forecasting has been recognized.

The need for understanding a future trend, the need for a forecast, is not limited to foreign policy. In economics, and in certain branches of sociology, in population science this need has been recognized for 150 years. After all, Malthus was forecasting the future trends of population growth. Today leading demographers, as, for instance, F. Notenstein of the Princeton Institute on Population and one time of the League of Nations, were and are forecasting future population trends. Precise methods are applied—results are verified *ex post facto*, after the forecasted years come. Population forecast is important for our economy and politics. Forecasting in economics is done by a number of scholarly institutes and by leading economists—for instance, Colin Clark. Professor Seymour Harris of Harvard is forecasting the number of college graduates in America in twenty years to come, while other sociologists predict success in marriage,[56] increase or decline of divorce rate, increase or decline of delinquency,[57] numbers of the mentally ill, or even success in probation in cases of individual delinquents. No one has ever questioned forecasting and preparation of military strategy. In 1906, the former chief of the German general staff, von Schlieffen, prepared the famous Schlieffen plan. Part of it was the attack on the right wing, against Belgium. Already in the 'twenties memoranda were written in the German general staff on partition of Poland and creation of spheres of influence between Russia and Germany. For centuries men were dealing with problems of the future, preparing for war. Today, more than ever, we need new techniques of forecasting in our efforts to prevent war and build peace, an international order governed by law.

[56] Ernest W. Burgess, Leonard S. Cottrell, *Predicting Success or Failure in Marriage*, New York: Prentice Hall, 1939; "Prediction of Adjustment in Marriage," *American Sociological Review*, 1936, pp. 737–51.

[57] Hornell Hart, "Predicting Parole Success," *Journal of the American Institute of Criminal Law and Criminology*, Vol. XIV, November, 1923; Sheldon and E. T. Glueck, *500 Criminal Careers*, New York, A. Knopf, 1930; and many others.

In foreign policy, forecasting, is far more important today than before. It is enough to glance at the map of Europe and history since 1939. Understanding of our future is today a matter of survival.

Functional Theory of International Politics

Foreign policy is a function of domestic policy, and in turn the domestic is a function of the foreign. It is impossible to divorce foreign policy from domestic; they are both inter-dependent. Hitler's domestic policy was shaped by his for-eign political objectives—he was building war industries, training armies, streamlining the human mind for warfare, cruelty and conquest. Factors of his foreign policy objectives were domestic. To build up an economic potential for war, to adjust economic, military and other already known factors, he had to build them up at home. At the same time, Hitler's "domestic" objectives were to make the Germans a privileged race "Herrenrasse" to rule foreign nations. His domestic aim was to expand German industry and enrich Germany by spoliation of foreign nations, just to mention a few of his do-mestic objectives. All of those "domestic" objectives deter-mined the foreign policy.

Activities, often crucial for an international politics de-cision, have an internal, domestic character. In a proper analy-sis of international situations and international politics, we cannot draw a line between domestic and international. The study of international policies is, I should say, of a marginal character because of the mutual interdependence of foreign and domestic politics.

It is usually difficult to translate this functional relation-ship into a causal. It is very hard to prove that the domestic policy is the cause and the foreign is the effect of domestic policy or vice-versa. Usually both policies of a government are so strongly interrelated that a simple causal sequence can hardly be used as means of explanation because we usually have a reciprocal and even simultaneous causation. Foreign policy is the cause of domestic policy, and vice-versa, domes-tic is the cause of the foreign. We usually discover an interdependence, which we call function, and which, if translated into causal relationship, might have the character of mutual simultaneous causation.[58]

Foreign, as well as domestic policy is not an abstract phenomenon. Both depend upon a large number of factors, such as economic and social organization of the country, distribution of economic and political power, idea-systems, general cultural background, as well as geographic position and natural resources. All these elements condition the domestic as much as the foreign policy of a government.

A government represents the views of a certain party or parties; it represents interests of a group or a number of groups of one social class or a number of social classes. In a fascist state, the character of a government, the way it operates, is no secret, the ruling group is well defined and even conspicuous, and the ideology and objectives are usually stated. In a truly democratic country, even a conservative government may reconcile a number of interests, such as industry and agriculture. Regardless of the type of government, in an analysis of foreign policy, we need to ask these questions: (a) What kind of interest does a given government represent? (b) For whom? In whose interest is the foreign policy made and what objective is chosen? (c) What is the function of foreign policy? What is the government trying to achieve by its conduct of foreign policy within the general framework of its activities?

Such an approach we may call a functional one since first we try to discover a functional relationship or interdependence between the domestic and international politics, which are as a rule interrelated, secondly we try to discover the function, the role of foreign politics, its objectives within the context of the whole framework of government's activity.

The functional theory is the premise for a forecast. As foreign and domestic policies are functionally interdependent, changes in foreign policy are reflected in domestic. Foreign policy decision, transformed into action becomes a social process; we observe this process and it forms the basis of our

[58] See Chapter III: *Causation.*

forecast. Before action is taken by a government, a state, against another one, a number of factors must be adjusted for—in other words, preparation for an aggression can be observed. Adolf Hitler and Mussolini, before starting their wars against Ethiopia, Czechoslovakia, and Poland adjusted a number of factors: instead of consumer goods, industry was turning out capital goods—armaments; the military draft was extended or compulsory military service reintroduced by Hitler; paramilitary organizations such as the S.S., S.A., Hitlerjugend, Fascist militia, and others grew in number and military training was introduced in the schools; transportation was adjusted to future warfare; development of air transport, air-force training was emphasized; alliances against prospective victims were prepared (alliance with Hungary and Poland against Czechoslovakia, with the Soviet Union against Poland), to mention only a few; Mussolini addressed a crowd at Palazzo Venezia with a gun in one hand and a book in the other. His address changed into a scream, the crowd into a mob. It was an appeal for war, conquest to come, an appeal covered up with platitudes. A Nazi leader promised hysterical German crowds guns instead of butter. Masses were whipped up to a frenzy, to mass hysteria, so that they could be easily pushed into a war. In times of mass armies, masses must be first conditioned, before they can be used for aggression. The process of conditioning (hate campaign) might be observed before an aggression starts. Germany's heavy industry was in swing—steel mills on the Rhine and in Silesia were turning out heavy armaments day and night. Hitler was not preparing guns, tanks and divisions in order to play a soccer game against the well known Czechoslovak soccer team. The trend of Hitler's policy was evident. So was the trend of Mussolini's foreign policy. The trend could be discovered through study of ideology, through observation of domestic policy, change of factors, observation of initial courses of action. Those "initials" indicate the policy decision, direction of the trend. Identification of a trend, of its direction, is already a foreign policy forecast.

After the end of the Second World War in 1945, both the

United States and Great Britain hastened demobilization. Armies were brought back from the continent to the United States; G.I.'s returned to their work and swelled the student rolls in colleges, while leaves of tropical plants covered the bombers and fighters with the green of peaceful oblivion, somewhere in the Pacific islands. The warships were put into mothballs. Industry changed its production instantly from tanks to automobiles, frigidaires and air conditioners. Daily papers, lecturers in women's clubs, teachers in colleges, preachers in churches argued for peace and cooperation, praised goodwill of the Soviet government. The Soviet government, however, in reality did not demobilize its army. On the contrary, large new armies in the satellite countries were drafted, trained, indoctrinated; consumer goods did not appear in quantity on the Soviet market; capital goods were and are turned out in secrecy; no information can be secured through accepted channels; the simplest economic information is veiled in secrecy. No secrecy is necessary in a production for peaceful purpose. Even simple, statistical data are hardly available and, once they are given, their veracity is challenged by facts. At the same time, the government of the Soviet Union wages a number of wars by proxy—in China, Korea, Greece, and Indo-China—releases a policy of cold-war in the Balkans and Europe, combined with camouflage-tactics-peace propaganda, Stockholm appeal flying on the false wings of a Picasso pigeon. The factors of Soviet domestic policy, present foreign policies as well as communist ideology, justify a hypothesis of an aggressive trend.

The analysis of factors and the observation of changes in domestic policies forms the empirical basis for our foreign policy forecast. Changes in domestic policies reflect the build up of factors for foreign policy objectives.

Alternative Situations

A foreign policy forecast is in consequence an identification of a trend, direction, of social actions and a hypothesis of purpose, objectives. Forecast is not a prophesy. Forecast is solely a hypothesis, mostly a weak hypothesis, not a certainty.

Should we suggest a forecast, let us be careful, restrained, modest, and, above all, cool, with emotions under control. As there is no certainty we anticipate not one, but many alternative situations. Not only *a* may happen, but also *b, c, d, e,* and *n.* The process of forecasting is in principle inductive, especially in its initial stage.

TABLE XII

Foreign Policy Forecast

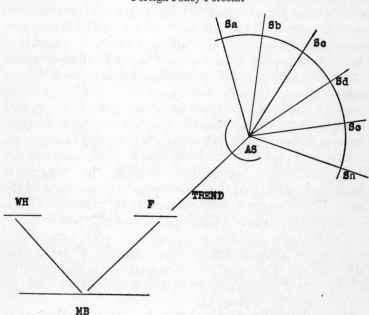

WH — Working Hypothesis

MB — Main Body of Facts: factors, policies, objectives (ideology; changes in domestic policies).

F — Forecast (Trend)

AS — Alternative Situations

$S_{a \cdots n}$ — Situations

A graph describes visually our thought process. We start with a working hypothesis (WH), from general knowledge of facts, that the Soviet government's objective is a farther expansion. With this hypothesis we attack the main body of facts (MB) available to us, such as continuous build-up of military strength, anti-western propaganda, absorption of satellites, production of armaments—factors which were mentioned before. We study now the factors reflected in changes in domestic policies, objectives. Here comes our foreign policy analysis based on three concepts: factors, policies, objectives (ideologies) related to problems and situations. Facts were selected, and they provide a basis for an inference, conclusion: trend is toward expansion. This conclusion represents a higher level of approximation, the level of finding. This is our forecast (F). The whole process is an operational method —from a working hypothesis we proceeded with our selection of facts to an inference. Our inference, forecast, indicates a trend. But a trend may produce not one, but many situations (S); it gives a government which released the foreign policy not one, but many alternative choices of action. There are alternative situations (AS), S_a, S_b, S_c, S_d, S_e, S_f . . . S_n. Each alternative situation which we may expect as a result of the trend of Soviet policies may suggest a number of alternative policies. A Soviet analyst may view Western policies in a similar way. He may also suggest alternative situations and alternative policies. But, let us admit this is a rather complex, maybe too complicated, proposition.

The alternative situation approach was and is applied in foreign policy analysis. This method was applied by men of various political views for various political purposes. Hitler's decision to attack the Soviet Union was probably based on an assumption that once Great Britain was defeated or close to collapse, the time had come to attack the Soviet Union. It seems that this was his conviction rather than anything comparable to a hypothesis. His ambassador to Moscow, Schulenburg, was however more experienced. Schulenburg's analysis was based rather on an hypothesis and alternative situations.

Here is an example of his way of thinking, taken from a tele-
typed memorandum of April 28, 1941.[58a]

". . . We must distinguish between two possibilities:
  a) England is close to collapse. If we accept this, Russia
     is no potential ally of the English;
  b) if we do not believe in the immediate collapse of
     England, then the thought might suggest itself that
     by the use of force, we must feed ourselves from the
     Soviet territory."

Schulenburg's term, "potentialities," corresponds to our alternative situations. He wrote further, "A German attack on
Russia would only give the British new moral strength." This
forecast was certainly correct.

The "Unexpected" Situation

Of course, even an elaborate method of foreign policy forecasting may fail. It may fail because of an error in theory,
method of analysis, method of operation,[59] false or unknown
facts, erroneous inference. An analyst may overlook alternatives, or suggest too few. It is hardly possible to anticipate all
possible future situations. Accidents are situations which
were not anticipated, or could not be anticipated.

The risk of error in foreign policy forecast is of course high.
The risk is present in every research—as was already said—
and a contingency for error takes care of that. In foreign
policy forecast the risk is higher, the contingency greater.
This should be stated clearly in every forecast, and result in a
greater modesty, restraint, rather than in an "I know it better"
attitude. In a foreign policy forecast a number of possible situations favor a wide arc of probability—within a contingency
of error.

Error, accident, unexpected events, and failure of proper
identification of a trend—all are against a forecaster. Is the
whole effort worth while—since the chances of failure are as

[58a] *Nazi Soviet Relations*, p. 333.
[59] See Chapter I. Scientific Approach (*Operational Method and Method
of Analysis*).

high or higher than chances of success? The very effort of coping with problems of the future trains us for it, helps us to understand the vital and coming issues. It prepares us also for effective actions and balanced decision in unexpected situations which may require spontaneity. Generally, it prepares us psychologically and may improve our chances of success. We use the same method in its initial stage, the same alternative approach.

In a regular foreign policy analysis, our attempt is to find out what *is* happening *now*, what is the *present* situation. The next stage—policy formulation—is concerned with alternative policies, which can be applied to cope with an existing problem situation. Forecasting goes a step further. We ask ourselves in what direction *the trend is moving*; how the situation may change in the future; how the problem may develop in the relatively near, not in the distant future; what alternative situations may arise. The process of foreign policy analysis and foreign policy formulation is put that way into a perspective of both past and future.

Statesmanship and Foresight

How far shall we look ahead? As long as a foreign policy trend is followed, the thought process is empirical and factual. The trend is usually closely connected with the immediate, present situation, with the situation within this month, this year—maybe the next one or two. An analysis of an observed foreign policy can hardly advance beyond the time limits which are contained within the very nature of the trend. The past and present facts are the foundation of our forecast of Soviet policies in China, India, Korea, Europe. A statesman must, however, look further. His forecast becomes foresight and foresight is statesmanship. A statesman looks a generation or even two ahead; his outlook considers a time-space necessary to create conditions of international security and social advancement for those to come. His concern is not solely the immediate, but the fate, the destiny of his nation, of mankind, the future of the very basic values we cherish. He must look far ahead, understand the future, and no one who lacks this quality deserves the name of a statesman. Statesmanship requires singular qualities. Research and foreign policy analysis cannot, unfortunately, provide all necessary elements, which would give power of understanding such a distant time-space, although an ability to apply scientific method might be essential. Here enters the role of broad vision, imagination, ideas, even phantasy, those creative elements of thinking, which escape precise definition and description.

CHAPTER VIII

Scylla and Charybdis

-1-

THE overemphasis put on certain methods (rather on techniques) at the expense of our scientific curiosity about environment, social phenomena and problems, may have a destructive effect on a discipline. It may detach a science or a discipline from its vital function, divert interest from crucial problems to irrelevant, or even to insignificant, episodes which have the dubious value that they fit perfectly into a clever scholastic scheme.

That has happened to a small number of American sociologists. Overemphasis on quantitative methods, statistics, has led to the point that the stress on detail and hair-splitting has beclouded our understanding of the great trends and problems of our society.[60]

[60] Carl Sauer, the well-known California scholar, in a brilliant article criticizes the present trends in social science. "American Social Science," writes Sauer, "has indeed become a dominant folkway to associate progress with putting the job of inquiry into large scale organizations, under formally prescribed methods, and with limited objectives. Having adopted the name 'science' we are impressed by the 'method of science' as inductive, quantitative, experimental. We are even told that this is the only proper method. . . . Statistical and experimental procedures are, however, tools, limited to certain purposes, and dependent as to product upon the quality of the problem that has been set up." That way the scope of science, contrary to its very sense, argues Sauer, is limited "by what may be measured." No field can be defined by method. The present trend involves a risk of confusing means and ends, industriousness with intellectual achievement. Carl O. Sauer, "Folkways of Social Science" in *The Social Sciences at Mid-Century*, Papers Delivered at the Dedication of Ford Hall, April 19–21, 1951; published for the Social Science Research Center of the Graduate School by the University of Minnesota Press, 1952, p. 101.

C. Wright Mills, in his introduction to the Mentor edition of Thorstein

Of course statistics have their important place as a device of fact-collecting and comparison, but they are not the sole avenue to truth. Often it is not applicable, sometimes misleading. In fact, the perfectionists of the quantitative schools have sometimes confused, on the one hand, ends and means of science and on the other, techniques, with methods and theory. Science simply does not equate with certain types of techniques.

From a group of scholars comes also a warning that mechanical projection of concepts of physical sciences into the field of social studies may lead to an error. Problems of values are of such significance in the latter, that it changes the character of inquiry. To this group belongs the known economist F. A. Hayek, the author of *Counter-Revolution of Science*.

At the other extreme are those (mostly natural scientists) who negate entirely any significance of the scientific method in social sciences. The super-sceptics argue that the scientific method has little if any application in the study of human society. We may call them pyrrhonists of social science, since they tend to deny the possibility of application of scientific methods in the study of society.

This division can be noticed, not solely among scholars. It can be noticed in different color, intensity, among the general news reader, in public opinion. The atomic discovery, the threat of an almost inter-continental war has shifted hopes of many from technology and natural sciences to social and political sciences. They expect a solution from social and political sciences and from wise leadership. Successes of sciences in physics, medicine, will, they hope, give us the same success in solving human problems. Public opinion is not a

---

Veblen's *The Theory of the Leisure Class*, New York; the Mentor Book, 1953, p. x, discusses the "higher statisticians" in the social sciences who, as he says, have trivialized man and society. On the other hand anti-intellectualism and reaction against scientific inquiry has appeared. Merle Curti writes about: "distrust in many circles of the scientific method itself as an instrument for guiding men out of chaos and darkness into peace and light." "Human Nature in American Thought: Retreat from Reason in the Age of Science," *Political Science Quarterly*, Dec. 1953, p. 507. This distrust is felt above all in the realm of social sciences.

monolith—it is divided. Fear, insecurity, have also released an aggressive feeling, an anti-intellectualism—the other extreme in this dichotomy.

The problem of the place of method in social sciences has become a key issue of American sociology today. The study of international relations and foreign policy, being a part of social sciences, faces a similar problem and is part of a similar controversy.

— 2 —

Science has advanced through changes and advance in method and theory. Changes of methods and in consequence changes in theory are milestones in the history of science. New facts mean little, unless their meaning is understood. The understanding of new facts is made possible thanks to new methods and theories. But method does not exist without content, purpose. Method is a result of our attempt to solve problems and to understand the nature of things. Methods and theory in bacteriology made the knowledge of facts scientifically effective, as much as advance in physics, advance in theory and methods, made the facts of the atom an effective part of science. The problem we face here is not theory and scientific method "to be or not to be"; it is not a problem of rejection or acceptance of scientific thinking; it is solely a problem of a proper use of proper methods, proper theory, even proper techniques; it is the problem of our compass, of the purpose of science—which should not be lost in obsession with certain, definite methods or techniques. The purpose, objective, of research, the discovery of truth about real problems, should guide our method, and the method, technique, should be applied only whenever it is necessary, and in a way which leads to understanding of relations between facts, to the discovery of approximate truth.

— 3 —

Not so long—only ninety years—ago, medicine was regarded as non-scientific, as an art rather than science and application to science. Similar arguments to those we can follow today in social sciences and in study of foreign policy were discussed by fathers of modern medicine, among them Claude Bernard. Do we have any doubts today about application of scientific method in medicine? But ninety years ago, indeed, it was different.

In February, 1877, Claude Bernard outlined a book on medical science—a work of 28 years.[61] In this classic work *Principles of Experimental Medicine,* Claude Bernard still had to fight for a place for medicine as a science and its application, as contrasted to medicine solely as an art. Bernard opposed those who saw the terminal point for medicine at that time in what he calls "l'empirisme"—a concept different than our "empiricism." By "l'empirisme," Bernard understood a routine of observation of the sick, of disease and application of various medications, without an effort toward creation and application of a science. As our social and political technicians refuse sometimes to recognize the need for a science of human society, so did the medics of pre-scientific medicine. Bernard said about them: "if an 'empiric' physician (médecin empirique) lacks scientific sense, which would make him conscious of his ignorance, he will necessarily fall into *'non-scientific empirisme'* (*l'empirisme non scientifique*) and will become a charlatan." A whole chapter is devoted to "the false idea of those who believe that a physician should never go beyond *'l'empirisme'* because it is an art and not a science."[62]

Another chapter is entitled *"L'empirisme non scientifique engendre la médecine de fantaisie et favorise l'ignorance et le charlatanisme."* Observation, facts, alone, without theory and method, are not science—this was his argument, this was his opposition to non-scientific "empirisme."[63] In his earlier

61 "Plan Nouveau de mon Livre" in 1947 Edition: Claude Bernard, *Principes de Médecine Experimentale,* introduction et notes par Leon Delhoume, avant-propos par Leon Binet, Paris: Presses Universitaires de France, 1947, p. XXIII.

62 op. cit., p. 48.

63 ". . . l'empirisme n'est rien autre chose qu'une sorte d'expérience inconsciente et comme instinctive acquise par l'habitude et par la pratique même des choses" (op. cit., p. 44). Bernard uses the term "empirism" for a concept different from our empiricism—which is a part of scientific method based on induction. Today, many technicians in politics, international relations, follow this type of empiricism.

volume, *Introduction to Experimental Medicine* (*L'Introduction à l'étude de la médecine expérimentale*) published as early as in 1865, he felt that, "The future of experimental medicine depends on creation of a method of research, which could be applied fruitfully to the study of phenomena of life. . . ."

Such were the beginnings of modern, scientific medicine, which is rather a recent discipline—the same struggle against the super-sceptics and against the "super-scientists." Similar problems of statistics—"it can be useful," he wrote, "but it is not any basis of experimental medicine," it "can supply empirical data (results) but it is unable to give scientific results." Scientific laws—not statistical—give us understanding, explanation of phenomena.[64]

He discusses statistics with full understanding, emphasizing its utility, especially when facts are simple. And here are the "super-scientists." He wrote in December, 1865 about "the fanaticism of physico-chemical preciseness which is detrimental to physiology and medicine," although it is useful in physics and mathematics.[65]

Students of medicine in Bernard's classes devoted a substantial part of their time to study of method, scientific method, to discussions of concepts—such as observation, experimentation, hypothesis, verification, conclusion; in short, theory of science. A large part of his classic "Introduction" devoted to problems of method and theory, is a philosophy of science which could be taught today, not necessarily as a part of a course in medicine. The study of those abstract concepts, abstract though rooted in experience, was a foundation of studies of early scientific medicine.[66] It was this method which gave the vigor to *science* of medicine and unusual results.

Claude Bernard was a philosopher of science and a great natural scientist, one of the founders of experimental medicine and biological sciences. He emphasized the significance of method and theory—but he was not obsessed with it. He

[64] op. cit., p. 62, 63, 67.
[65] op. cit., XVIII.
[66] op. cit., p. XXXVI.

saw differences between scientific synthesis and techniques. He knew the limitation of the method, of the system—understood the marginal areas of creative chaos, and the danger of "super-scientism" as well as of the other "pyrrhonists,"—the super-sceptics.

— 4 —

A scientific inquiry—in social sciences, international relations—moves between the Scylla of super-scientists and the Charybdis of super-sceptics. Paradoxically, both have made contributions: the perfectionists, as they have shown the limit of our techniques; the super-sceptics, as they challenge issues of limits and limitations of science, and remind us about the existence of a non-scientific area of human experience, significance of this area, especially that of a moral order and also of the incomprehensible in human motivation.

Methods, techniques, should be applied without a dogma, which would impose a rule that only a certain kind of technique or method is an index of science. New techniques are continuously developed. Various types of inquiry may require various techniques, methods, theories. Not always do we need the whole elaborated mechanism. In study of foreign policy we may concentrate sometimes on study of factors, sometimes on ideologies, objectives,—other times on policies. Such is the case in study of present distribution of power in Europe—it is a study of factors. The weight may shift from one factor to another as, for instance, in a study of distribution and trends of political power in the Soviet Union, a problem of significance for future peace. The emphasis of an analysis is in this case on the social-political factor. Never should we stretch facts to a theory or squeeze phenomena into a system. Always looking toward facts, toward real social processes, policies, actions—we shall draw the inferences from them, and develop such tools, such approaches which give us a better understanding.

Nor is a form of a study alone a test of scholarship. Significant contributions were made in study of international relations and sociology by authors who did not follow a set system of rules in their writings, who followed their methods of analysis without making the reader aware of it, and who wrote brilliant essays in simple and understandable language.

Always elastic in application of our techniques and methods, never dogmatic, we shall keep a sober criticism toward our own effort and see the limitations.

The analysis of foreign policy is a research—an observation of human behavior, of social behavior—and methods should help us to observe, understand, infer, and make our findings. "I am a secretary of nature," said Claude Bernard. So are we secretaries, of the nature of human behavior in international relations.

At the end of our discussion, we may perhaps return to the problem of the very purpose of a scientific method in social sciences and in foreign policy analysis.

The choice of objectives of a foreign policy, as it was reiterated, is not scientific. It belongs to another area of human experience, to our economics and economic values, to political philosophy and to our ethics. True, the scientific method helps to make a proper, intelligent choice. The quality of science itself, however, is instrumental. It is similar to a tool. It can be used for various goals, for various purposes; for good or bad. A knife may be used to kill a man, as well as to perform an operation and save his life. Bacteriology may be used by men to prevent an epidemic; it may, however, also be used for bacteriological warfare. Once science is isolated from the very basic moral values it becomes extremely dangerous, it may become a veritable Frankenstein.

Similarly, a scientific approach to foreign policy is of like quality, and relations between morals and practical politics are similar too.

The separation of politics from moral goals of mankind is a dangerous proposition, a proposition which sooner or later leads to conflicts. Politics, without moral principles and without moral restraints is like a boat without compass and rudder. It is politics without any moral direction. One of the basic moral premises in relation to the individual, is the principle of mutual aid and the rendering of help to the weaker, as well as protection of the weaker against the stronger.

Similarly, in international relations the protection of weaker nations as well as individuals against the power of the stronger, and the principles of mutual aid form a premise of an international morality. In modern history—in spite of devastating and cruel wars—there are hopeful signs of such a development in international politics. International help in times of famine, such as aid given to India, to China, to Russia, and the activities of the Red Cross and United Nation agencies in giving immediate help to the population of the Philippines in order to prevent a famine after a plague, as well as the aid given by neighboring nations to Holland during a recent flood, all are evidences of mutual aid. Since the time of Woodrow Wilson the general and consistent trend of democratic foreign politics has been directed toward a world which would outlaw war as an instrument of national policy. in spite of wars, in spite of other conflicts, such is the consistent trend, continuously reemphasized by such official acts as the Covenant of the League of Nations, the Geneva Protocols, the Briand-Kellog Pact, Atlantic Charter, United Nations Charter, North Atlantic Treaty Organization and many other treaties and conventions. The great, strategic objective of the democracies is a free world under law, free of misery, war and slavery. Maybe it is a vision, a social myth, but it is an image which must direct our deeds for the very sake of our survival, and it is a moral image with a fair chance to become reality.

However, democratic foreign policy in order to be effective must be realistic in the empirical sense. Situations must be evaluated as they really are, not as we wish to see them. Policies toward our goals must be realistic in this very empirical sense. It means, in other words, that policies must be supported by adequate factors, that they have to be evaluated in concrete situations as they really are, with cold, scientific, unemotional evaluation of the situations.

Scientific method, a careful analysis of a situation will give us a better chance to make proper choices in our effort to make this world safe for democracy and, above all, safe for the individual.

Index

Abramovich, R., 13
Abrams, Frank W., 122
Absolute values, 120
Affirmatives, 14
Air-force, 114
Almond, Gabriel A., 122
Alternative approach, 138, 143, 148
Alternatives, 136
Alternative situations, 161
Ambivalence, 62
American Academy of Political and Social Science, 84
Anti-Stalinists, 13
Anvil (operation), 151
"Apparatus," 48
Approaches, 31
   alternative, 138, 143, 148
   area, 24
   functional-interactional, 35
   method-centered, 21
   problem-centered, 21
   "problem paper," 134
   problem-solving, 17
Arctic, 100
Area approach, 24
Astakhov, 150
Atomic powers, 114
Atomic weapons, xv
Axiom, 7

Bacon, 14
Bailey, Thomas A., 122
Baldwin, Hanson W., 152
Beard, Charles A., 77, 78
Beck, J., 5
Berle Jr., Adolf A., 48

Bermuda Conference, 151
Bernard, Claude, 7, 14, 170
Biological needs, 58
Black, Max, 11
Bolyai, 8
Borgese, Giuseppe, 89
Bridgman, P. W., 43
Brookings Institution, 46, 47, 121, 134, 138
Brookings staff, 52
Brooklyn College, 41
Bukharin, N., 60

Capitalism, 36
Carr-Saunders, 112, 113
Catholicism, 37
Catlin, George, 58
Causal-functional interpretation, 37
Causation, 22, 31
Chamberlain, William H., 5, 13
China, 104
Chinese Communists, 9
Churchill, W., 5, 151
Clark, Colin, 157
Clausewitz, 130, 131
Coale, Ansley J., 112
Coexistence, 22
Coincidence, 30
Commitments, 54
Committee to Frame a World Constitution, 88–89
Conant, J. B., 8
Concepts, analytical, 48
Concepts, ideological, 63
Conclusions, 6
   level of, 9

175

Conflict, 22, 25
Conflicts of interests, 26
Congress party, 60
Context situation, 128
Contingency, 6
Cooperation, 22, 25
Correlation, 30
Cousins, Norman, 122
Cultural idea-system, 61, 89
Cultural pattern, 109, 119
Culture, 57, 119
Curti, Merle, 168

Dallin, D., 3
Definitions, operational, 43
Dehumanization of politics, xvi
Department of State, Foreign Service
    Institute of, 42
Diplomacy, 123
Doctrines, 79, 89
Documentation, 10
Dogma, 8
Dragoon, 151
Dulles, 152
Durkheim, 63

Economic Cause, 33
Economic factors, 103
Economic interests, 60
Economic potential of China, 104
Effects, alternative, 37
Eisenhower, President Dwight D., 81
Empirical method, 3
Empirical realism, 4, 14
Error, 6, 14
Euclidean mathematics, 7

Factors, 48, 49, 50, 51, 94
    economic, 103
    geographic, 97
    military, 113
    moral, 114
    population, 108
    social-political, 116
    social-psychological, 123
Facts, 16
    relationship of, 15
    selection of, 10, 14
Feller, A., 85
Findings, 6
    level of, 9

Finletter, Thomas K., 122
Forecast, 155, 161
Foreign affairs, 70
Foreign Policy, 4, 50, 55
    Aztec, 58
    definition of, 44, 50
    objectives of, 48
    United States, 33
Foresight, 165
Fowler, H. W., 137
Functional Theory, of international
    politics, 158

Galileo, 8
Gallup, George, 122
Geographic factor, 97
German-Soviet cooperation, 129, 149
Gibson, Hugh, 44, 46, 130, 156
Gideonse, Harry D., 115
Goals:
    strategic, 128
    tactical, 126, 128
Governments-in-exile, 111

Hamilton, 77
Harris, Seymour, 157
Haushoffer, 98
Hayek, F. A., 168
Henderson, Loy W., 44, 47
Herodotus, 119
"Hierarchy of importance," 12
"Historical mission," 83
Historicism, 62
Hitler, 9, 10
Hoffman, Paul G., 122
Hopi, 42
Huntington, Ellsworth, 100
Hutchins, Robert M., 122
Hypothesis, 6, 51
    level of, 9

"Idea a priori," 7
Idea-systems,
    political, 61, 89
    cultural, 61, 89
    relationistic, 88
Idealists, 84
Ideography, 64
Ideological objectives, 90
Ideology, 48, 50, 51, 57, 61, 63, 64,
    71, 117, 121

India, 9
Individual, in society, 61
Inductive procedure, 49
Industrial capacity, 114
"initials," 160
Inquisition, 37
Integration, 24
Integration of Social Sciences, 24, 25
Interdependence, 37, 159
Interest, 89, 90
International conflict, 25
International cooperation, 26
International politics, theory of, 158
International relations, xiv, xvi, 49
    philosophy of, 87
Interrelationship, 27, 128
Irrational element, 73

Jefferson, 77

Karpovich, Michael, 72
Kennan, George, 84
Kirk, Dudley, 112, 113
Kirk, Grayson L., 23, 124
Kiser, Louise K., 112
Knowledge, Sociology of, 16
Kuznets, Simon, 118

Lake Forest seminar, 138, 139
Language, 40
Laswell, Harold D., 123
Law, international, 50
Leaders, 117, 123
Leadership, 123
League of Nations, 27, 112
Lenin, 60, 130
Levitas, Sol, 13
Limitations, 4
Lobatschevski, N. I., 8
Lord, Mrs. Oswald B., 122
Lorimer, Frank, 113
Luxemburg, 104

Macaulay, 14
Machiavelli, 132
MacIver, Robert M., 36
Mackinder, Sir Halford J., 28, 97
Mahan, Alfred Thayer, 78, 97
Malinowski, Bronislaw, 11, 41, 42, 96
Malthus, 157
Mannheim, Karl, 16, 71, 88

Manpower, 103
Mao, 9, 11
Marx, Karl, 25, 28
McCloy, John J., 115
Mead, G. H., 29
Meinecke, 76
Method, 169
    operational, 18
Method-centered approach, 21
Method of Analysis, 18
Military factor, 113
Miliukov, Paul, 72
Mills, C. Wright, 167
Mixed processes, 22
Mongol Khutuktu, 59
Monistic, 31
Monocausal, 31, 32
Monroe's doctrine, 79
Moral factors, 114
Morgenthau, Hans, 29, 84, 97
Motivation, 58
Movements, totalitarian, 132
Munich, 5, 10
Myths, social, 66, 67, 73

National committees, 111
National interest, 53, 75, 78, 84, 89
Negatives, 14
Neutrality, 22
"New Leader," 13
Newsholme, S., 112
New Testament, 37
Niebuhr, Reinhold, 122
Nikolayevsky, B., 13
Notenstein, Frank W., 112, 157
Nuremberg, 10

Objectives, 49, 50, 51, 57, 79, 89
    hierarchy of, 83
    strategic ideological, 90
    tactical, 90
Observation, 4
Ogden, C. K., 42
Oil, 106
Opium War, 33
Opportunism, 5
Orthodox Palestine Society, 72
Overlord, 151

Palmer, D., 85
Papacy, 59

Parallel, 7
Pareto, Vilfredo, 32, 35, 37
Pasvolsky, Leo, 134, 137
Pavlovsky, M. N., 59
Pearson, Karl, 34
Pilsudski, Joseph, 62
Planning, 45
Pluralism, 31, 32
Poincaré, 15
Poland, 62
Policy, 49, 50, 51, 54, 126
  Planning staff, 156
Political behavior, 119
Political, idea-system, 61, 89
Political science, xv
Politics, use of alternatives in, 148
Population factor, 106, 108
  Over-population, 59
Power, 86, 114
Power realism, 4
"Prime-mover," 31
Princeton University, 112
Principles, 55
Problem-centered approach, 21
"Problem Paper" approach, 134
Protestantism, 36
Public opinion, 78, 122

Quantitative methods, 167

Radek, K., 60
Raison d'état, 40
Realism, 4
Realists, 84
"Relationistic" idea-system, 88
Relative values, 120
Religion and science, 8
Ribbentrop, 83
Richards, I. A., 42
Rieman, G. S. B., 8
Roberts, Owen J., 122
Rogers, Lindsay, 78
Roosevelt, Franklin D., 137
Roper, Elmo, 122
Russia, 28

Sapir, E., 42
Sauer, Carl, 167
Sazanov, Serge, 72, 73
Schlieffen plan, 157
Schulenburg, 163

Schuman Plan, 96
Science and religion, 8
Scientific method, 173
Scientific research, 107, 114
Scientism, 155
Scope, 3
Semantics, 39
Sequence, 30
Situations:
  alternative, 161
  unexpected, 164
Social Causation, 27
Social change, xv, 84
Social forces, 75
Socialization, 61, 120
Social-political factor, 116
Social Process, 22
Social-psychological factor, 123
Society, the individual in, 61
Solutions, 66
Sorel, Georges, 71
Sorokin, Pitrim, 35
Soviet policy, 10
Sparkman, Senator John, 85
Specialization, 24
Stalin, 28, 60, 128
State Department, 45
Statesmanship, 165
Statistics, 171
Steel, 104
Strang, 149
Strategic goal, 128
Strategic-stage objectives, 128
Strategy, 126, 128
  concept of "stages," 128
Survival, biological, 110, 111
Symbols, 40

Tacitus, 119
Tactics, 126, 128
  as camouflage, 133
  objectives of, 90, 126, 128
Taeuber, Irene B., 112
Taft, Donald R., 25
Tawney, R. H., 35
Terminology, 39, 52
Theopolitics, 59
Theory, 19, 20, 169
  functional, 158
Third Rome, 72

Thomas, Norman, 85
Thompson, Warren S., 113
Tibet, 9
Torricelli, 8
Totalitarian governments, 133
Totalitarian movements, 132
Totalitarian systems, xv
Totalitarian tacticians, 133
Truman, Harry S., 82
Truth, 6
  objective, 18

Underdeveloped areas, 143
Unexpected situation, 164
Uniformity, 120
United Nations Statistical office, 113
Universal Military Service, 38
Universal values, 120
University of Virginia, 41
Uranium, 106
Utopia, 71
Utopianism, 67

Values, 13, 16, 58, 59, 65, 75, 88, 93, 120
Variables, 23
  isolation of, 35
Variability, 120
Visions, 66, 71
Viviani, 8

Wars, causality and study of, 31
Weber, Max, 35
Webster, 64
Weltanschauung, 62
Wheeler-Bennet, John W., 10
Whitehead, Alfred N., 11
Whorf, B. L., 42
Wilson, Woodrow, 33
Words, meaning of, 39
World federalists, 89
Wright, Quincy, 31, 122

Znaniecki, Florian, 38, 93